Farewell
to
Beantown

P. Marie

Farewell to Beantown
Copyright © 2018 by P. Marie
Cover Design: Nativesons Designs
Editor: Kate Benson @ Chasing Sophie Publications
Copy Editor: Patricia Korbet @ PK Designs
Formatting: PK Designs Editing and Graphics
ALL RIGHTS RESERVED.

Dedication

Cynthia Ann Lebretore
March 21st, 1964 – January 2, 2018

The Boston Belles series was written about the unconditional bond of friendship and family. This story is dedicated to a friend who recently passed away from cancer. She kept her friends and loved ones close, always smiling and laughing leaving them with memories to ease the sadness once she left this earth.

Her bond of friendship with Kirsten, Diane and Julie was one that most of us search for all our lives to have. Cindy left behind the love of her life, her husband, Tom, along with her mother, sister and brother, who will take her legacy and carry it forward in several charities in her name.

Cindy, every time I see a cardinal or the color purple, whether it's in the swirl of the sunrise or sunset, I will always think of you. You may not be here on this earth, but your memory will live in our hearts forever.

Rest in Peace.

Prologue

While the pallbearers carried her body to the gravesite, I glanced out the window of the limousine lost in my thoughts.

What would happen if the rain falling started to seep into her casket? Would she get cold? Was she watching from above, scared knowing she was unable to get out?

Morbid as these thoughts were, they caused me to panic.

I felt a hand grab mine and gently squeeze, all at once pulling me from my anxious thoughts and calming me. Turning, I gave Frankie a nervous smile, returning the small gesture, comforted in knowing he understood the reason for my silence. Once the casket was in place, the funeral director walked over and opened the limo door, extending his hand to me. I took it slowly stepped out, my heels sliding into the ground, making my legs feel like weights and matching the sinking feeling in my stomach as Frankie gently held my elbow and led me to where she would forever rest.

Looking around, I was amazed to see how many people had come to pay their respects to this woman. They say in life you never really know how many people you've touched until you're gone. The sea of people here was a true testament to her legacy.

Staring off into the crowd, I showed no emotion, but inside I wanted to scream and cry for all I had lost.

I would never have the opportunity to show her all I would accomplish. She would never see me walk down the aisle or be happily married. Most of all, she would never see the children I would raise in a home full of love, strength and happiness. These were the things I'd always wanted her to be a part of, but now she will only be a distant memory.

As the ceremony began, someone handed me a single rose and as I held it, I rubbed the stem, resentful when I found it smooth instead of the searing pain I'd expected from a stray thorn. I needed to match the pain I held in my heart.

The priest greeted the crowd that formed around us, beginning the ceremony by opening a small bottle and pouring dirt in the shape of a cross over the top of the casket.

"Unto Almighty God, we commend the soul of our sister departed, and we commit her body to the ground, ashes to ashes, dust to dust."

Drifting in and out of my thoughts, I only caught pieces of what the priest was saying. The faces surrounding me were all a blur until I came upon Angus, Colin, Mikey and Joey, all standing in line with their hands folded in front of them, heads bowed in respect. I knew without even turning around that my two best friends were directly behind me in support of my loss. Throughout all of this, they'd never left my side, not even for a minute, and I thanked God each day for bringing them into my life.

Frankie took my hand and gestured for me to place my rose on the casket and whisper my final goodbyes before our guests could follow suit. His grip tightened on me as I bent down, giving me the strength that I needed to get through the moment.

Knowing this would be the last time I would ever be with her, I kissed my palm and placed in on the cold, wet wood and released the breath I'd been holding for days.

"May your soul finally rest in peace," I whispered and dropped the rose into the darkness, watching it settle against the concrete slab where she would remain for eternity.

Chapter One

One month earlier...

Lexi

As we touched down in Boston after getting the call about Nonna, we hurried to gather our belongings and headed to the hospital. Upon arriving, we were all met by Mama T, her features exhausted and worried as she filled us in before taking Frankie and Gia down to see her. Watching them walk away, I was unsure as to what the next couple of days would bring.

Colin suggested we grab a quick bite in the cafeteria to give them time alone as a family. My heart said no, I wanted nothing more than to be there for Frankie, but I knew this was what they needed. We'd just settled at our table when my phone chimed with a new text, pulling my attention from the group.

> **Hey, I stepped out for a bit and didn't see you in the waiting room.**
>
> *Sorry, we thought we would give you some time alone as a family.*

We are in the cafe.

Okay, we will be right down. They are taking her for X-rays to check her lungs for fluid.

Are you okay? Is she going to be alright?

I will be once I see that gorgeous face of yours. Honestly, Lexi, I don't know. She is so weak and frail looking. I am worried. She is struggling.

Taking in his words, I began to choke up. Nonna had become someone I called family and to lose her would be devastating to us all.

Several days came and went with everyone chipping in by cooking and bringing food. However, when Colin needed to fly back home to take care of his business, you could see the sudden change in Gia.

It was nice watching her let guard down and lean on him for strength. He was the calm she needed to ride out this storm. Mikey and Joey kept the office running, checking in daily while Shelby kept in touch each night. With all the support Frankie,

Gia and Mama T had, it allowed them to each take turns staying with Nonna while the others went home to regroup.

When it was time for Frankie to have his turn at the hospital, he asked me to come with him so that we could be together. Our time was spent sitting in a nearby chair or on the edge of the bed beside her watching the sports channel while she slept. Although she dozed in and out, she seemed to be getting stronger each day, giving us faith that she'd pull through.

We had no idea how much weaker her heart had become.

Frankie

Fucking A ... when did I turn into a pussy? I thought to myself as I wiped the stray tear and swallowed the pain that came from watching Lexi sleep beside Nonna, holding her hand.

This girl had so much love to give, never looking for anything in return. Things like this were where I questioned whether she should be with me or find someone else who could give her the life she deserved. Pops always told me, *'If you treat your girl with the same respect and love as your mother, you will never spend a night alone.'*

I never knew what that meant until today. I would give Lexi the moon if she wanted it.

As she started to stir, she lifted her head and gave me the most beautiful smile, turning me inside out all over again.

"Hey, sleepyhead," I said, leaning in to kiss her cheek.

"Hey yourself," she whispered.

"You and Nonna both were snoring up a storm over there." I chuckled. "I had to turn up the volume on the TV, for God sakes."

"Kiss my ass, boy. I don't snore," Nonna said, opening her eyes.

"Oh, sorry. It must have been my imagination." I smirked. "You might want to wipe the drool mark off your cheek, old lady."

Reaching towards her cheek, she made a swiping motion and gave me the finger.

Yep, she was getting back to normal.

"Listen, why don't you two pains in my ass take a walk and get out of here for a while? I don't need you people tucked up my ass twenty-four seven." She rolled her eyes "Frankly, I am getting tired of you watching me breathe. Go home and leave me be. I am fine."

"You know what, cranky ass? I think we *will* head out for a bit and get some fresh air," I said, lifting from my place in the chair and smiling down at her. "Is there anything your highness requires while we are out?"

"Yeah. Peace and quiet, so get the hell out and don't hurry back," she said, making a waving motion with her frail hand. "Oh! Bring me back an éclair."

"Okay, you two. That is enough." Lexi clapped her hands. "Nonna, we will leave you alone, but just for a little bit," she said, kissing her cheek. "If you promise to behave while we are gone, we will sneak you in that éclair."

I grabbed her hand, dragging her off to spend some time alone and give Nonna a break. We walked, taking in the fresh air and busy streets of Boston until we found a quiet spot in the local park under a large oak tree. I was unwrapping our lunch when I noticed Lexi had grown quiet and wasn't acting her usual self.

"What's the matter, Lex? You seem off."

"Just been thinking," she started, glancing at me with a worried look. "I want to ask you something, but if I do, please be honest with me, okay?"

"Sure, babe," I said, giving her a reassuring smile. "I can promise you one thing with you and me. I will always tell you the truth."

"Why did you choose me over Paige?" she asked, her voice small as she stared down at her lap. "She is already established in life, has a great job, she's good looking and from what I can tell, doesn't come with drama like me."

As her words hit me, I couldn't help the shock that came with them. It was all so out of left field, but her features told me it wasn't the first time she'd had her doubts. I knew then I had to set her mind at ease once and for all.

"Lexi," I started, hating when she glanced away from me. "Hey, look at me," I continued, finally pulling her eyes to mine. "Listen, I'm not gonna lie to you and say Paige isn't all those things. She's a great girl, but Lexi, she's not you, sweetie," I confessed, the surprise in her features not missed on my part. "You're beautiful. You're strong. You're the most caring person I've ever met, and in you, I've found my best friend and the one only person I've ever truly loved," I whispered, squeezing her hand in mine. "I have no idea where this relationship is heading, but I do know I'm not going to throw this away. I'm going to do everything in my power to make sure we stay just like this because my heart knows exactly what it wants and that's you."

11

She stared back at me teary-eyed for a moment, searching my face for any signs of doubt and finding none, jumped in my lap and pulled my lips to hers.

"Frankie Moretti," she whispered, resting her forehead against mine once she pulled away. "You are everything I want and more. You have made me realize what love is and I want to have that every day with you, too." With a final kiss on my lips, she released a sigh and pulled away, jumping up and moving to a stand. "We'd better get back to Nonna," she said. "Gia is supposed to take the supper shift, and I am not too sure Nonna will allow any of us to stay much longer. Besides, we need to get her that eclair or she will have a nutty."

"Okay, but I hope you don't think you can jump on my lap and kiss me like that and think we won't be finishing this conversation naked later," I said, adjusting myself.

"Oh, just wait," she giggled, pulling my lips down to hers before swiping her tongue over my mouth. "You think Tom Brady's got moves?" she asked, releasing me before winking over her shoulder. "You ain't seen nothin' yet."

When we made it back to Nonna's room, I glanced inside to find Gia brushing her hair, taking care in putting it back in her signature clip. Stopping short, I gestured for Lexi to look. No matter how relentless those two were at being smart asses to each other, seeing this would melt the coldest of hearts. It was just another example of the unbreakable bond my family shared.

"Hey, dick face," Gia said, pulling me from my admiring thoughts with an eye roll. "It's about time. Nonna was going to call the police if you didn't get back here with her éclair." We watched her hop off the side of the hospital bed, bumping me playfully with her elbow as she shot Lexi a wink. "Where the hell'd you go? Stop off for a little *nappy time*?"

"Cut the shit and stop being a dick, Gia," I said, stepping inside. "We went to the park, had lunch, and then we went to get the goodies for Nonna."

"Whatever." She shrugged, reaching for the bag and scowling when I held it over her head. "What's in the bag? I am starving."

"Sorry, sis, but Nonna first." I walked away, setting the biggest éclair on Nonna's tray. "Once she's done, you can have whatever you like."

"Frankie," Nonna said, taking a bite and releasing a groan. "I have to say you are my favorite grandson."

"I am your only grandson, smart ass." I laughed, shaking my head and grabbing the Boston crème donut, my sisters favorite, out of the bag and smiling at her as I took a big bite.

Lexi

After a week, Nonna was discharged, and she couldn't have been more excited to get home. I watched Frankie help her out of the car and into the house, her weakness making her struggle, but she was also determined to do it on her own. Swatting Frankie's hand, she took slow but steady steps, showing us all she was not ready for the reaper just yet. Frankie stepped back giving her space, but also close enough to make sure he was there if she stumbled. Mama T was holding her oxygen tank and hose walking alongside her while Gia stayed directly behind her, the three of them forming a perfect triangle of protection.

"I can't wait to have a plate of spaghetti," Nonna announced as she made her way slowly to the door. "I think that place killed my taste buds. The shit they call food would make pigs puke."

"Ma, I will have a nice dinner ready for you if you promise to rest," Mama T said, leading her into the house.

"Theresa, I have been laying down long enough. My ass is numb, and even my wrinkles have wrinkles. Just let me sit in my chair and watch TV. I If I doze off, leave me be, for Christ's sake."

"Listen here, chickie," Gia said, patting her on the ass. "Your surgery is dependent on how strong you get. You need to rest and eat to get to where they want you to be so they can operate. Can't you just cut the shit for once and listen to us?"

"Hate to tell you, Nonna, but they're right. It's for the best," Frankie said, holding onto her arm. "You're gonna have to buck up, old woman. Besides, the nurse will be here daily checking on you and doing therapy to build up those muscles."

"Great! Another asshole to boss me around," she complained, plopping herself in her chair, exhausted from just the short walk and getting annoyed with the oxygen hose for tangling.

As I watched this tennis match of words, I couldn't help but laugh at them. Had they not realized she'd do what she wanted when she wanted? Nonna had never been a woman to let others dictate her life, and even I knew she'd be leaving this earth on her terms. Not even God Himself would have a choice in the matter if she had her way.

"Okay. Everyone out," I announced, making a sweeping motion with my hand. "Nonna needs to get settled, you two need to catch up on paperwork, and I need to help Mama get started on those meatballs."

"Oh! Look who found her balls." Gia winked. "Our little Southern belle gets a little Moretti injection and thinks she can boss us all around."

Her statement left me speechless, but Frankie and Mama T were quick to whip their heads around.

"Gia!" they said simultaneously, Mama's voice coming out in a shout while Frankie's resembled more of a protective growl.

"Thank Christ!" Nonna chimed in as she settled into her chair behind us. "It's about time he dipped his wick into something decent. Good for you, Lexi."

Nonna's words shocked me in ways Gia could only dream of. I felt my eyes go wide as they met Frankie's cocky smirk, my hand clamping over my mouth as the loud laugh left my chest.

You couldn't make this shit up, but I'd found out early on that being a part of this family meant taking the good with the bad. I wouldn't have it any other way.

"Well," Frankie sighed, pressing his lips to my forehead. "Guess our little secret is out."

Gia spent dinner staring at her phone, smiling and rapidly typing back text after text. Frankie and I knew who was sending them, but before we could give her shit about it, Nonna served her up some sass.

"Bella, seeing your face stuck in that phone of yours during dinner, one can only hope it was that Irishman texting you," Nonna said, never lifting her eyes from her plate of pasta.

"Um, yeah sorry," she replied, shoveling the last bit of pasta into her mouth. "He wants to come back up here and just told me he's going to bring his dad."

"Mama, Angus is awesome. Just the sweetest guy ever. You have to meet him," I said before diving into his background, telling her all about how he'd lost his wife to cancer and built a business while raising Colin on his own. She listened intently, gripping her chest with compassion in respect to his sacrifices. A quick glance at Frankie told me perhaps I'd been a bit too enthusiastic, but I wasn't sure why. It wasn't like I was trying to fix them up or anything. I just thought they'd get along well.

"Well, I like meeting new people," she said, clearing the table. "From what I saw of Colin while he was here, I am sure we will get along just fine." I returned my attention to the last of my dinner, cringing when her voice returned to ask the one question I'd been avoiding. "So, Lexi, but will you be staying here in Boston for the summer or are you going back home?"

As everyone focused on me, I couldn't help when my face began to flush.

"I've been kind of wondering the same thing," Frankie admitted, pulling me closer. "Not to sound like an asshole or anything, but I wish you'd stay here. What she put you through was ridiculous, Lexi. You don't need that kind of stress."

"Well, if I'm honest, I was trying to avoid it altogether," I admitted, glancing away in embarrassment before peering up at Frankie. "Any idea when the brownstone will be ready? If it's soon enough, maybe I can just move in there, and I won't have to be a burden on anyone."

"Lexi." Mama waved me off. "You know you're more than welcome to stay here. Besides, it would be a big help. We could always use the extra help with Nonna."

"Thank you," I whispered, grateful beyond words. "I'll need to go home to grab some things and see my dad again since school will start back in a month."

"Of course," Frankie said, kissing my temple in reassurance. "I just ask that you wait for me to fly down with you. We can stay with your parents or in a hotel, but there's no way I'm leaving you alone with that barracuda for a second."

"Okay." I nodded, relaxing against his chest, knowing I'd be protected. *Too bad it's from my mother*, I thought, swallowing hard before standing and gesturing toward the living room. "Let me just text my dad."

> *Hi Daddy, can you call me tonight when you get a chance? Frankie and I want to talk to you.*

> **Sure, baby girl. Is everything okay? I am just finishing a**

meeting I should be free in about an hour. Is that too late?

Nope perfect. Thank you, Daddy. I love you!

Love you more, baby girl.

Frankie

After speaking with Jackson, I was amazed at how quickly he agreed to Lexi staying here.

Something just didn't sit right with this whole situation between Lexi and her mother. Why did Jackson not step up like a father should and stop that bitch from hurting their only child? It just didn't make sense. If he wasn't such a great guy, and Lexi didn't adore him, we would have had words a while ago. One thing I knew for sure was that her mother was a twat, and I would not have her fucking with Lexi's head anymore. She had enough stress with all these unanswered questions from the attack, the threatening texts, and let's not forget Craig. Sadly, the elephants in the room were Jackson and Caroline Cole and why her mother was so evil to her only child.

Although you could hear the sadness in her voice that the conversation was one she had to have with her father, you could also see the tension lift away when her dad agreed it would be best for her to be here until school started. Jackson assured me that staying with them would not be an issue, and he would speak to Caroline to ensure a pleasant visit. I hoped so, because, as much as I was raised to respect women, I refused to take any shit from that broad.

After a long ass day, all I wanted to do was lose myself in Lexi, so that's exactly what I did. After making love, she fell asleep in my arms sated and happy. I smiled to myself, admiring her innocence but grateful she was slowly coming out of her shell.

Lexi

I laid on Frankie's chest with my eyes closed and pretended I was sleeping, never having felt so content in my life. We shared a connection in Montana that I could not explain. It happened again tonight. It was as if our movements were synchronized and we became one. They say the difference between making love and having sex is that making love is felt deep in the soul, and tonight, I felt mine explode. Shutting my thoughts off, I fell asleep peacefully in the arms of the man I love.

"Morning, beautiful. Time to get up," Frankie said, kissing my forehead and pulling back the covers.

Instantly, I was afraid to open my eyes because I realized where I was.

"Holy shit, Frankie!" I whispered harshly, vaulting off him in a panic, grabbing my clothes and trying to get dressed as quickly as possible for my inevitable walk of shame. "Your mother is going to kick my ass to the curb when she realizes I slept in here!"

Laughing, Frankie grabbed my arm and pulled me back into his chest, causing me to stumble and fall on the bed with me on top, straddling him.

"Relax, Lexi. It's too early for anyone to be up, no one will know you stayed in here," he whispered, grinding his crotch into me. "Besides, I'm not quite done with you yet."

When we finally made our way downstairs for breakfast an hour later, I was surprised to find Gia's eyes already on me.

"Lexi, come here. I want to see if you have a fever," she said, placing her hand on my forehead. "I think you might be a bit delirious."

"What are you talking about?" I asked stepping away and looking at her as if she had ten heads. "I feel fine."

"Oh, okay." She shrugged, popping a bite of toast into her mouth with a smile. "I was just worried. It seems you lost your way last night and ended up in the wrong room."

Mortified, I looked around the kitchen to find Nonna smirking as she read the paper, Mama's shoulders shaking with laughter at the sink, and Frankie sitting on the stool like the cock in the hen house.

"Leave her alone, Gia," Mama said, her grin wide as she dried her hands on her towel and kissed my blazing cheek.

"Yeah," Frankie chimed in, resting his arm on my shoulders. "Stop being a dickhole."

"Gia, there will come a time when all your bullshit talk will bite you in the ass, my dear," Nonna said, shuffling back toward her room. "I, for one, can't wait to watch."

I was about to say something in my own defense, but my phone chimed, saving me.

"Good morning, Shelby," I said, holding my phone up so she could see all of us. "You called at the perfect time."

"Well, if I waited for you two asses to reach out, I would be dead." She smirked. "How's Nonna? What's going on there?"

"Jumpin' Jesus Christ, I am fine, Shelby!" Nonna mumbled as she shuffled down the hall. "Great. Now I have them haunting me from Montana."

"Nonna is doing well, as you can hear," Gia said from behind me. "She is resting and getting stronger."

"Hey, sweetie." Mama T waved.

"How is the ranch coming along since we left? You ready for guests?" Frankie asked, resting his chin on my shoulder so he could see Shelby.

"Yes, sir. We have our first six quests arriving this week, and it looks like we are booked solid 'til January." She smiled. "My parents are hiring a couple of extra hands since I am heading back in a couple of weeks. I need to get my schedule set and books and stuff ready for school."

"Yay! I can't wait to see your ugly mug!" Gia yelled from the sink.

"It's strange. I don't feel bad leaving this time. Christian is coming back to help and to see Sara. It seems the manager they hired back at his farm is working out great, so he has free time on his hands to visit here."

"Awesome! The brownstone just needs a few touch-ups, and we should be able to move the furniture and everything in storage by the end of next week," I said, looking to Frankie for confirmation.

"Yes, ma'am. It will be ready for move in by the time you get back. I will have Mikey and Joey get the shit from storage. You can FaceTime them with where you want stuff, and Lexi and Gia will help."

"Great!" Shelby clapped before looking back at me with concern. "Lexi, are you heading home soon?"

"I am, but only for a visit. Frankie and I are heading back next week to grab my stuff, and then I am coming back here to help with Nonna."

"Is your mother okay with that?"

"Shelby, after what she pulled, she is lucky I'm going back at all."

"I understand, Lex." She nodded. "You have to do what's right for you. Gia and I have your back," she promised, warming my heart. "Okay, guys. I hate to run, but I need to get my shit done before my sister's start squawking. Kisses bitches."

"Bye, Shelby!" we all yelled in unison before watching her go.

I ended the call, my smile fading when I saw the text alert from an unknown caller. I slipped my phone into my pocket, silently hoping my nerves didn't show on my face as my heart began racing.

I couldn't catch a break.

Frankie

After hanging up with Shelby, Lexi excused herself to use the bathroom and hurried off.

"Hey, Lexi?" Gia yelled, following her up the stairs, "Use this!" she ordered, tossing her a can of air freshener. "I don't need to smell what you had for supper last night down the hall."

"If I didn't love you, I would punch you," she said, disappearing behind the door.

I finished my coffee as I checked my emails, wondering what the hell was taking Gia so long and why Lexi was still in the bathroom. Being away and not putting in full days had me up to my ass in paperwork at the office. Thank fuck for Mikey and Joey. They'd more than earned their piece of the partnership over the last few weeks.

"Gia, get your ass in gear and let's go!" I called up the stairs. "I have a shit ton of work to do at the office, and I have to meet Paige at the rental property."

"I am coming, ya fuck stick. Jesus! You don't have to yell," she griped as she came down the stairs, texting like a mad woman

"Is Lexi still in the bathroom?"

"Yup, she must have the shits." Gia laughed. "I knocked and told her we were leaving, and she said goodbye, so let's go before you have a stroke."

Hoping she was okay as I stared up the stairs for a moment, I cursed the time when I realized I was already late and had to leave.

"Okay," I whispered, more to myself than anyone else. "I will just shoot her a text when I get to the office."

Lexi

I needed to act normal and excuse myself to the ladies' room without anyone noticing I was in a panic. Sitting on the toilet with my hands shaking I opened the text.

He will throw your ass to the curb once something prettier

23

**comes along, so don't get too
comfortable staying there.**

My stomach began to turn, causing me to gag until, finally, I emptied the contents of my stomach. Who was this person and how did they know I was staying here with Frankie? I knew I couldn't hide this from him and the police. The last time I tried, he lost his mind. I decided it would be best to wait until he got home so we could discuss this together without ruining his entire day. I was doing my best to calm my nerves when I heard a sharp knock on the bathroom door.

"Hey! Lex, we are leaving," Gia said sounding a little concerned. "Are you okay?"

"Yup, just doing my business," I lied, saddened that years of practice had made it so believable. "Have a good day. I'll see you tonight."

"Okay," Gia said, her voice low. "Use the spray. I can smell you out here."

Chapter Two

Frankie

I was nearly through the mountain of paperwork on my desk when I realized I had not texted Lexi. Grabbing my phone, I typed my message quickly, hoping she was okay.

> **Hey, gorgeous. Just checking in. I didn't get my kiss goodbye this morning, and I am all out of whack. I need me some sugar!**

A few minutes later, my phone dinged with her reply.

> *Sorry, sweetie, I promise to give you extra sugar this evening. My bad.*

> **See you around six. Think of me today.**

> *I think of you always. Be safe.*

She must be busy with Nonna, I reassured myself once I saw her clipped messages. Looking at my watch, I checked the time and knew I needed to grab some lunch before meeting Paige, cringing at the latter, but knowing business was business. I could only hope she remembered that. Closing my office door, I noticed Gia was having a video chat with Colin in the conference room over lunch. Unable to pass up the opportunity to offer Lexi some vindication after seeing how she'd made her squirm, I walked in, gesturing for Colin to stay silent while I stood behind her, watching her flirt up a storm.

Time to play bad ass brother.

"Well, when you do come, I will make sure I ask for some time off. That way, I can show you around Boston. I would love to have your dad meet my mom and grandmother," Gia said as she glanced up at the screen, oblivious to the fact I was in the room. "He will just love them."

"That sounds good, but I was also hoping to spend some time alone with you," he confessed, shooting her a wink. "I miss my girl."

"Oh, honey," she batted her eyelashes. "By the time you get back to South Carolina, your balls will be hitting your knees." She chuckled, righting her expression. "I told you. You gotta earn Maggie."

Oh, my God, I thought to myself as she gestured at her crotch. *I think I just threw up in my mouth.*

"So, Maggie, huh? That's what you call it?" I said, making Gia sit up straight as her face went pale. "TMI, Gia. TMI." I tsked. "Stop using my equipment for your lame sex tape and get back to work," I ordered. "As for you, *partner*, get those orders filled. We've got a business to run here."

When I arrived at the brownstone, I found Paige outside, holding the paperwork I was waiting on while she texted on her phone.

"Hey, Frankie." She smiled, moving closer in an attempt to hug me. "How are you?"

"I am fine, Paige," I said politely, offering her my hand professionally as I gestured toward the binder she was holding. "I don't have a lot of time. Is that the paperwork I need to sign?"

"Umm, yes," she said with a nod, obviously surprised by my reaction. "Why don't we go inside and take care of it so that you can leave? I know you're busy. I also have a check here for first, last and the security deposit from the other tenant's parents," Paige said handing me a nice fat check as I signed the last of the lease agreements.

It seemed as though the girls would have another set of students from Boston College next door for the year. Unlike most property owners, I happened to love students because most were spoiled rich kids and their parent's money made my bank account a lot happier. The construction industry could be fickle, but rich kids would always need a place to rent.

"Thanks. Let's hope they don't trash the place," I said, taking it from her. "I am leery about renting, but I don't want it to sit idle and cost me money."

"I wouldn't worry," she said condescendingly. "The background checks we did show they are members of some pretty prominent families here in Boston."

"Perfect." I smiled. "Since you're so confident, and your property management team is in charge of keeping an eye on them, I'll hold you responsible for making sure that's true."

I hated being a dick, but I learned the hard way not to shit where you eat.

I was turning to leave when she grabbed my forearm, pulling my eyes back to hers.

"Wait," she said. "I heard Nonna was in the hospital," she managed nervously. "Is she going to be okay?" My eyes moved to her grip on my arm, prompting her to quickly remove it. "Listen, I know we're not together anymore, but I still like to think I'm your friend. There's still a place in my heart for you and your family."

"She's doing well. We're waiting for her to recover a little further before her operation, but Lexi's helping out… keeping an eye on her," I answered. "Thank you for asking."

"I thought Lexi would be going back to Charleston?"

Her disappointment wasn't lost on me.

"No." I shook my head. "Lexi's staying with me until the brownstone's ready," I admitted, cutting the conversation short when I realized I'd given her more information than I'd intended. "Anyway, if we're done here," I said, glancing down at the binder, "I should get going. I've got a few more sites to visit."

"Yes, we're done," she said, shaking her head clear before handing me the binder. "I am sorry to have taken up so much of your time."

As I slipped back into my truck, I was grateful the meeting had gone better than I'd expected.

Hopefully, she was finally taking the hint.

Lexi

After getting the text message, my entire day was ruined.

I'd spent the better part of the day trying to figure out the best way to tell Frankie about it, hoping he wouldn't explode because I'd waited so long. Eager to distract myself, I spent time with Nonna, watching television and making supper.

"Bella, what is going on in that head of yours?" Nonna asked as we cut vegetables for dinner. "You're a million miles away."

"Oh, nothing. I'm just lost in my thoughts today, Nonna," I said, hoping she would drop it.

"Lexi, I can tell there is something you're holding back," she insisted, popping a carrot into her mouth. "We don't have to talk about it, but you know keeping shit inside will fester and make you sick."

"You just focus on getting stronger and stop worrying about me," I said, offering her the best smile I could manage.

"Well, if you change your mind, I am here if you need to talk," she said, kissing my cheek before heading toward her bedroom. "There's not much this old body can do anymore, but I can listen."

Deciding to take a stand, I called Officer Walsh to tell him what happened. Not only did I think it would help my stomach stop churning with nerves, I thought it might help ease the blow later for Frankie if I'd already spoken to the authorities. However, when Walsh's voicemail came over the line, I couldn't deny I'd been relieved to not have to speak with him directly.

I left him a quick, descriptive message asking him to return my call, and as I hung up the phone, I felt like a weight had been lifted. I was determined to not allow anyone else to control my life ever again.

Frankie

Once I was finished checking on the projects I'd been neglecting all week, I headed back to the office to find Gia, Mikey and Joey working in the conference room. While I'd be the first to admit my sister was a real pain in the ass, having her here had been a godsend.

Since she enrolled at Boston College, I'd been covering her tuition and telling Ma I was just helping fill out her student loan forms. Once Gia graduated in three years, I knew I would tell her the truth, but for now, I was happy letting my mom think I was a good son and brother. The bottom line would always be that my father had created a business, and we'd made it profitable. Keeping secrets was never something I wanted, but I had to do what was best for the family.

Thankfully, it had paid off.

"Nice to see you all working instead of fucking off, for once," I said, plopping myself down in the cushy chair.

"Well, big brother, we didn't really have a choice," Gia sighed, gesturing toward Mikey and Joey. "It seems these two assholes forgot to get me the permit information so that I could have them pulled, and now, we are behind."

"Shut your hole, Gia," Mikey said, gathering paperwork and placing it into folders. "It's no big deal, bro. She can pull them tomorrow, and we will be ready to start. She just needed to bitch. You know how she gets if she can't bust balls at least once a day."

"She's right, Mikey." I shook my head. "She should've had this shit two days ago, but we blew it off, so stop giving her shit for doing her job," I said. "You've been pissed off ever since she chose Colin over you, and it's enough."

"No," he started, his chest puffing out in frustration. He was about to say more, but Gia cut him off.

"Oh, whatever! I'm not having this argument again," Gia snipped, grabbing the last of the paperwork and standing in a huff. "Just get me the shit I need."

"What the fuck just happened, dude? How am I always the bad guy?" Mikey asked, rubbing his head before facing Joey and me. "I am just trying to make sure she doesn't get hurt. I don't want to see her get fucked when he dumps her. Partner or not, I'll kick his ass."

"Listen, Gia is an adult. Whether we like it or not, she can handle her shit. Come on. Let's wrap this crap up and get out of here. I am done for the day and want to see my girl."

Lexi

When Officer Walsh finally got back to me, he said the text messages were coming from a burner phone, same as last time, but to continue to inform him, so that we have them on record. He also said they'd received several anonymous calls with potential information on my attack, but because of the amount of the reward my father had offered, it would take time for the police to wade through each claim and eliminate the false ones. When I hung up, I felt a little better knowing they were doing what they could to catch whoever had been wreaking such havoc on my life.

I busied myself with dinner and smiled as I heard Gia and Frankie walking in a little later.

"Wow! It smells freaking awesome in here, Lexi," Gia yelled before running up the stairs to change. "I could eat the ass off a horse."

Laughing at her comment, I continued to stir the gravy for the roast when I felt two large hands grab my hips.

"I'm not sure what smells better, you or that roast." Frankie nipped at my earlobe. "But I can tell you I'm going to enjoy every bite of both."

"Hello to you, too." I blushed as he continued his assault on my neck. "I'm happy my cooking arouses you, but if you make me burn these biscuits, you'll be asking a Southern girl to commit a cardinal sin," I teased, pulling a growl from his chest as I bent and brushed my ass against his crotch.

"You're going to be the death of me," he said as he placed his hand over his heart, feigning pain. "If you won't let me have my dessert now, I hope dinner is at least close."

"Fifteen minutes." I smirked, waving him off. "Your mother is on her way. By the time you've gone upstairs to change and wash up, I'll have your dinner ready, master."

"Fine." He shrugged, pulling his shirt over his head to reveal his rippled abs, making me swallow hard as he playfully tossed his shirt at me and headed for the stairs. "Your loss."

Frankie

Watching Lexi in the kitchen caused my junk to stir. The way she stood there, her hips swaying back and forth, made me want to take her right there on the counter. However, with my luck, Nonna would have come around the corner and caught us in the act, giving me permanent erectile dysfunction. Even worse, Gia. There's no telling what the fuck she would have done.

I did know one thing. I needed to rein it in before I did something stupid.

Lexi

Over supper, I caught Mama T and Gia up on how Nonna did with the physical therapist while they were both at work, unable to stifle the laugh that came with remembering how unimpressed she'd been.

If she's just coming to make me move my arms in circles every day, she'd said. *She can find another patient because this shit is stupid.*

As the conversation wound down, Frankie decided enough was enough and stood from the table, gesturing for me to follow.

"Okay, ladies. You've had my girlfriend long enough," he announced, taking my hand and leading me away from the kitchen. "If you need us, we'll be upstairs watching TV."

"Yeah, okay." Gia snorted, elbowing Mama T. "And I guess TV is code for boinking?"

33

"Gia, leave them alone, for Christ sake," Mama said as she slapped her with the dishrag.

"You might want to listen to her and keep your mouth shut, Gia," Frankie warned with a cocky smirk. "These walls are thin, and unless you hurt yourself while you were talking to Colin on the phone the other night…"

"Oh, my God, Frankie! Shut up!" she railed, eyes wide with humiliation, making us laugh as I tugged on Frankie's arm.

"Come on, troublemaker." I shook my head, pulling him behind me.

"I'm about to show you, " he whispered with a devilish grin. "Just you wait and see."

I'd been lying over his bare chest, content with my fingers tracing over his abs, knowing I could stay like this for hours. Frankie had always been a patient and generous man when it came to me, and behind closed doors was no exception. Once that door was shut, Frankie was in charge, making sure we both enjoyed every second of our time together.

Sadly, I knew I couldn't put it off anymore. I'd have to tell him about the text.

"Frankie?" I whispered as I glanced up at him, finding him about to drift off to sleep. "Are you awake?"

"Yeah, babe," he murmured. "What's up?"

"I got another text today," I began, the words coming out in a rush.

Before I could say more, Frankie jackknifed from the bed.

"What? When?" he said, facing me with wide, angry eyes.

"This morning," I answered quietly. "I was—"

"Are you fuckin' kidding me? Why am I just now hearing about it?" he shouted, cutting me short as he stood and began pacing the room. "What parts of *you need to tell me* did you not understand?" I started to answer, but before I could, he cut me off again. "Lexi, this shit has got to end. We're together now. You should have told me," he insisted. "I know you think you're protecting me, but it's getting fuckin' old."

His voice rose enough to make my stomach flip with nerves, my initial instinct telling me to shut down, just like it had with Craig and my mother. That thought was enough for me to find my voice once and for all.

"If you'd let me talk instead of going all nutso on me, maybe I could fucking tell you," I snipped back, squaring my shoulders.

"Please, by all means," he said with a sweeping motion. "Fucking enlighten me."

"This morning when you were leaving for work, I got another text from an unknown number," I began, my chest still seizing in anger that he'd reacted so harshly. "Your hands were full, you were late for work, and whether you believe it or not, Frankie Moretti, I'm capable of handling some shit on my own, so I didn't say anything," I explained. "Instead, I called Officer Walsh and reported it while you were at work. I found out it was from another burner phone, most likely untraceable again, but he's looking into that as well as a few leads. Once they've weeded out the fakes, I'll have to go down to the station, and he promised to be in touch in the meantime," I said, my voice still clipped. "You were busy, I had it handled, and I kept my word by coming to you, so please chill."

A moment passed before he stepped back toward me, calmer.

"Look, I'm sorry I lost my shit, Lexi, but I'm not ever going to apologize for being protective," he said bluntly. "You've got to stop keeping this shit from me."

"I was going to—"

"You were alone in this house all day with Nonna." He cut me off quietly, my throat growing thick when I began to understand his side of it. "Whoever's watching you? They had all day to come here and hurt you both. I had no way to keep you safe."

"I'm sorry," I managed, my eyes moist with tears. "Frankie, I... I didn't even think about..."

"Shh, baby." He shook his head, drying my tears before returning to the bed and pulling me close. "Just no more secrets, okay?"

"Maybe I should go back to Charleston until this all blows over." I sniffed. "Maybe it's too dangerous for me to be here, Frankie."

"No, Lexi. You're not going back to that havoc. You're staying here, end of discussion," he disagreed. "I can't keep you safe there, but I can here. We just have to communicate. Don't worry. We're going to find out who's doing this, and they'll pay for what they've done. I promise."

I gave him a quick nod, composing myself and trying to calm my nerves. I'd nearly gotten there thanks to his palm running over my back when the deep laugh that slipped from his chest made me glance up at him. When I saw his expression, I rolled my eyes and smacked him.

"Are you serious?" I asked, glancing down at his crotch. "You're hard right now?"

"I'm sorry." He grinned, shooting me a wink. "That sassy little mouth of yours got Nick the dick all worked up."

"Well, I'd hate to disappoint Nick." As I yanked at his gym shorts and pulled them down, I said, "It feels like he could use a good tongue lashing."

Lexi

With our flights back to Charleston booked, I was happy when Gia said she was coming with us for *extra backup against the She-Devil* as she put it, but we all knew it was really so that she could see Colin. It worked out perfectly because I'd hoped she could be the buffer between Frankie and my mother.

"Lexi, I need help!" Gia yelled from her bedroom. "Colin just told me he's taking me on a carriage ride after dinner," she huffed, glancing up at me as I came to a stop in her doorway. "What the hell am I supposed to wear on a freaking carriage?"

"I thought you were coming for moral support?"

"I am, dear, but why should you be the only one getting laid?"

"Gia, would you shut your mouth, you brat?" I swatted at her. "Your mother is going to hear!"

"Oh, she heard you alright." Gia laughed, gripping her stomach. "We all did."

She was about to say more, but before she could, my phone rang. It was Shelby.

"Hello, ladies," she said. "Just calling to check in. I miss my girls."

"We miss you, too, Shelby," I said, looking through Gia's closet. "What's up?"

"Nothing. Christian's coming in tomorrow to help us get set up for the first wave of guests, but otherwise, I'll just be packing to come back to Boston," she said. "Can I tell you something? I love my family to death, but I can't wait to get back."

"I totally understand. As much as I miss Audrina, Carl and my Dad, after everything with my mother, I am glad I am here."

"Well, I for one can't wait to get out of this house," Gia bitched. "Unlike the two of you, I'm trapped now, but in less than a month, we'll all be in our own place and out of the dorms for good."

"You're welcome to come shovel shit if you need a break," Shelby said, swinging the camera to show us a wheelbarrow full of manure behind her. "Be my guest."

"Yes, or you could be living with the She-Devil, as you so affectionately call her," I offered sarcastically, laughing at her expression.

"I'll give both options a big, fat fuckin' no," Gia said, stuffing more clothes into her case. "Anyway, we'll be back in a couple of days. Frankie's got the meeting with Colin and Angus about some projects coming up, and Gia's just helping me pack up the last of my things."

"Sounds good. I've gotta go for now, but I can't wait to be back with y'all," Shelby said, blowing us a kiss. "Love ya! Mean it."

"Hey, you know what's funny?" Gia said, plopping back onto her bed. "Just a few months ago, Shelby was depressed and homesick, and now she can't wait to come back to Boston."

"I know the feeling," I admitted. "I was so afraid to come here and leave my family, as dysfunctional as they are, but meeting you and Shelby made me realize I was too sheltered and needed to experience life," I said, joining her on the edge of the bed. "I think now that her family will be okay with the ranch and with the extra help they can finally afford, it's different. She isn't needed there like she was before."

"Yeah," she said, twirling her gum as she stared at the ceiling before turning to face me. "Hey, did you hear her say she was sick of listening to her sisters?" she asked, making me nod. "Well, with everything happening here, I totally forgot about it, but back when we were in Montana, I was with Sara and Jodi in the barn helping out, and they said something I thought was weird."

"What was that?"

"Well, we were talking about boyfriends, and they brought up Shelby and how she was still struggling with the loss of Drew. When I asked who Drew was, they told me he was Shelby's boyfriend, and they'd been inseparable, but right after graduation, there was this tragic accident, and he died," Gia said with concern. "I tried to find out more, but when I asked, they clammed up."

"Wow, I had no idea," I admitted. "I guess it makes sense, though. She never wants to get close to guys or date anyone. She must be afraid of getting hurt again." I glanced back at Gia. "Well, she's obviously working through it in her own way. When she's ready to talk about it, she will."

"You're right," Gia said, lifting from the bed and looking out the window, deep in thought. "All of us have some piece of our lives we keep tucked away. Better than getting hurt again."

At that moment, I couldn't help but wonder what secrets she was holding in her own heart.

Despite the uneventful flight, I couldn't help my nerves. However, having Frankie and Gia with me gave me the courage I knew I'd need to get through this visit. As we pulled up to my parents' house, an uneasy feeling washed over me. After everything that had happened the last time I'd been here, I could never feel safe staying here again.

"You okay, babe?" Frankie asked, squeezing my hand.

"Yes," I said, giving him a shaky smile. "My parents aren't home yet. They won't be back from Savannah until late."

"Okay, peeps. Let's get this shit show over with," Gia yelled from the back seat. "We've got to get you packed and outta there."

Stepping out of the car, I looked up to see Audrina and Carl coming down the stairs to greet us.

"Ms. Lexi," Audrina said as she made her way over, engulfing me in her arms as Carl reached for the luggage. "We are so happy to see you."

"I missed you both so much," I said, hugging her back before releasing her, gesturing toward the others. "You remember Frankie and Gia?"

"I sure do." She smiled. "Welcome. It's lovely to see you both again. Now please come in. It's hotter than the devil's bath out here, and I have prepared a bite to eat and some sweet tea for you on the back porch."

Gia and I both followed her while Frankie helped Carl with the bags. As I stepped over the threshold and took in the familiar sound of the marble floors against the soles of my shoes, the gentle tap I'd remembered from my childhood did little to calm my nerves. There was something in the sound that tugged at my chest. My childhood home was exactly the same, polished and pristine, but something was off. While I couldn't identify it, I was left with a nagging feeling. Call it a sixth sense, but something wasn't right.

I brushed it off and followed Audrina to the back porch.

Chapter Three

Frankie

After having lunch and getting settled, we decided to head over to Colin's office to check on things. Jackson and Caroline would be back soon, and to be honest, I didn't feel like dealing with them just yet.

McGrath's Lumber office was small compared to ours. When you walked into the tight space, Angus's desk faced the door while Colin's sat across from him.

"Well, I'll be damned," Angus greeted us as we walked through the weathered screen door. "I asked the good Lord to show me the beauty in this day, and look what He brought me." He smiled, standing to hug the girls and giving them both a kiss on the cheek. "Colin, remind me to put an extra hundred in the offering plate this week at church for answering my prayers."

"Okay, old man. That'll do." Colin smiled, pushing away from his desk. "Get your ass over here, Gia. I missed you."

He reached for her, kissing her deeply enough to make her arms go limp, finally stopping when I cleared my throat.

"Once you're done mauling my sister, we've got business to discuss," I started. "We'll head out to the lumber yard, and the girls can help get this disaster of an office organized, so my orders don't get lost in this shithole."

"Good looking women and free help?" Angus laughed, smacking his desk. "I must've won the lottery."

I smirked, glancing over to find Gia staring up at Colin like he'd just shit a rainbow. Seeing my sister reacting like this to a guy was amusing, to say the least. Usually, she cut their balls off and served them for dinner.

"Okay, you three get out of here so we can file and get to work," Lexi said, glancing around. "Is there anything we should stay away from?"

"Honey, *mi casa es su casa*, have at it!" Angus said, getting up from his chair, ripped from years of use and squeaking with a sound of relief.

When I turned to close the door, I found my girl bent over Colin's desk, gathering papers. The sight of her ass in the air stirred all kinds of nasty thoughts in my head. The idea of playing boss and secretary at my office once we got back to Boston made me release a groan until the sharp sting of Angus' hand hit my head.

"Pay attention, son." He laughed, pushing past me. "We don't need you falling down the stairs and breaking your ass."

Lexi

I'd just slid the last folder into the cabinet when my phone rang, startling me.

"Hi Audrina," I said, settling into Angus' chair, exhausted. "What's up?"

"Ms. Lexi, there's been an accident," she sobbed into the phone, making me return to a stand so quickly, the chair toppled over, and Gia rushed to my side.

"What do you mean?" I demanded softly. "What accident? Who?"

"Your parents, Ms. Lexi," she sniffed. "They were hit head-on by a drunk driver on their way back from Savannah."

"Oh, my God," I gasped. "Are they okay."

"I'm going to get Frankie," Gia whispered, her words making me silently grateful as she moved toward the door to find him.

"I don't know, honey," Audrina's voice brought me back. "All the officer said was that I needed to contact their immediate family. They're in critical condition and being airlifted to Charleston Memorial. Carl and I will meet you there."

"Oh, my God," I sobbed, the weight of her words finally starting to hit me as I rested against the desk for support, barely noticing the shift on the other end of the line as Carl took the phone from her.

"Lexi, you've got to be strong, honey," he said gently. "Do you have a way to get there?"

"I... I, um," I stumbled over my words, searching for anything but coming up empty-handed until I saw Frankie come through the door. "Yes. Yes, I'm on my way."

By the time we arrived, my heart was beating out of my chest.

It seemed so surreal when it was your family. The last time we rushed into a hospital like this, it had been Nonna, and we had no idea if she would pull through. For the first time, I knew how Frankie and Gia felt—both walking in that night seeing her and when it had been me lying helpless—not having a clue what might happen. In the last few months, I'd seen my own fair share of tragedy and fear, but nothing could have prepared me for this.

Gathering my emotions, I found Audrina and Carl waiting for us, for the first time letting my feelings show as I rushed into their arms.

It wasn't long before the head nurse approached us, explaining my parent's injuries. Although they were both in surgery, it seemed my mother had sustained severe head trauma, so we wouldn't know how bad things really were until she woke up. However, as she led us to a private area reserved for families to stave off the swarm of reporters just outside, she'd promised to keep us updated and send the surgeon in as soon as they had finished.

We waited behind the door for hours, my mind moving in twenty different directions as I searched for any distraction. Gia and Colin brought coffee and made phone calls to Mama and Shelby while Angus paced the waiting room, excusing himself a few times for air, making me wonder if this was bringing up old demons for him. I tried my best to cling to the activity around us so that I wouldn't have to focus on my thoughts, but after a while, I relented and rested my head against Frankie's shoulder, staring off into space.

When the door finally swung open an eternity later, an older man in scrubs stood on the other side, his somber expression making my chest clench.

"Miss Cole?" he said, searching the room before finding my eyes. "Hello, I'm Dr. Burke."

I stood up despite my shaking legs and extended my hand, grateful when Frankie rose beside me, offering me the support I needed.

"I'm Alexis Cole," I managed, my eyes staring at him, silently pleading. "Are my parents okay?"

"Please, Miss Cole," he said, gesturing toward the seat I'd just spent what felt like forever in as he took the one beside it. Once we were settled, he finally began to speak.

"Earlier this evening, my team and I performed a craniectomy on your mother, which is a neurosurgical procedure used to help relieve pressure from the brain following severe head trauma," he began, reaching for my hand. "During the operation, she began to seize, causing her vitals to drop. We did everything we could to stabilize her, but unfortunately, we were not successful." He swallowed hard. "I'm very sorry for your loss. If you have any questions—"

"No!" I cut him off as I pushed his hand away roughly. "This has to be a mistake," I reasoned as I glanced at Frankie, his teary gaze making it so real, I forced my eyes shut. "She was just..." I snapped my eyes back open, the sound of Audrina's muffled sobs hitting me like a ton of bricks. "No."

"I can't tell you how sorry the entire staff and I are for your loss," Dr. Burke continued as he stood, his tone compassionate despite my outburst. "Your father has come out of surgery. He is expected to make a full recovery," he said, his eyes slightly lighter, giving my heart hope. "He's suffered a ruptured spleen, several broken ribs, and a concussion. It will take him some time, but as soon as he's out of recovery, you're welcome to see him," he offered, giving my shoulder an affectionate squeeze as I nodded numbly. "In the meantime, if there's anything we can do to help during this difficult time..."

"Thank you," I croaked, not recognizing my own voice as years of training forced my hand up to shake his, unsure of what else to do.

I'd just lost my mother. The same woman I'd fought to love me, who'd caused more hurt to my heart than any child should ever feel.

We may not have seen eye-to-eye, but she was the only mother I'd ever have.

I'd endure it all over again just to have one more chance to make things right between us.

When I turned around, I saw their faces—pity and sadness—staring back at me. I collapsed into Frankie's arms and cried until I had no more tears left to fall.

To this day, I could not explain the emptiness in my heart the night I lost my mother.

Numb did not describe it.

While Gia called her mother to give her the news, Colin booked Shelby a flight to Charleston. Mama T had to stay behind and care for Nonna, but I knew even through my heartache, she wanted nothing more than to be with me.

Angus played security guard, keeping the press away while we waited for my dad to come out of recovery. This was the darkest hour of my life, but even through that despair, I was proud to call these people family.

Waiting was torture, but I think even then I knew deep down I needed the time. I knew once my dad was brought to his room and I was allowed to see him, I'd have to be strong when I couldn't have felt further from it. The terrifying fact that I no longer had a mother kept slamming into me like a sledgehammer.

She'd never see me marry, watch me bear her grandchildren and raise them in a loving home. Despite our downfalls, I still held hope that she'd answer all the questions that had always tainted my heart. Only hours earlier, that had still been possible, but in an instant, one person's selfish decision had ripped it all away.

The wounds she'd caused would heal in time, but now, the mystery behind them would always remain.

When I was finally able to see my father, I clung to Frankie as we walked in, the situation reversed from several months before when it had been me in the bed, unconscious. Hearing the familiar beeping noise, I swallowed hard and stepped around the curtain to see the man I loved with all my heart covered in bruises, unconscious and helpless.

He had no idea that my mother was gone. It was my responsibility to tell him, but I had no idea how. I was the child. How was I ever supposed to tell my father that his wife was dead?

As I bent down and gently pressed my lips to his forehead, praying for strength, it was the first time I'd ever blatantly cursed being an adult.

"Daddy, I'm here," I whispered, grateful when Frankie took a step closer, giving me support. "Please wake up. I need you... I can't do this alone."

"You won't be alone, baby," Frankie promised, his lips finding my temple. "We'll get through this together."

"Frankie, he's going to be devastated," I whispered, my voice lost in the sob slipping from my chest. "I don't think I can do it," I managed, the reality finally hit me as I fell apart in his arms. "How am I supposed to do this?"

For the rest of the night, I could do little more than watch the rise and fall of his chest, thanking God he was still here, leaving one parent in my life to love.

A tap on the door broke me from my thoughts, and I turned to find Carl peeking inside.

"Ms. Lexi, I am sorry to bother you, but I wanted to let you know that Audrina and I are going back to the house. We need to inform the rest of the staff and keep the press at bay."

"Thank you, Carl. I'm not ready for that yet, but I don't want anything leaked until he's been told and has time to adjust," I said, reaching for him. "Please come in and see him before you leave."

Audrina stepped in a moment later, hugging me like she had when I was little and needed comfort most. Unfortunately, this time, there was no Band-Aid to fix my pain.

Eventually, Frankie and I fell asleep in the chairs waiting for my dad to wake up. The nurses came and went during the night, taking vitals and offering reassuring smiles that gave me hope time would heal all his wounds. Finally, at around eight in the morning, he began to stir, his heart rate spiking as the alarms alerted both the nurses and us.

The head nurse, Amy, came in and spoke softly, reaching for his IV.

"Mr. Cole, it seems you are finally going to wake up," she smiled at him as she injected the medication into the tube. "I don't want you ripping out those stitches, my friend. I am going to give you a little something to keep you relaxed." Looking him over, she wrote something in his chart and then turned to give Frankie and I a smile. "He'll be in and out for a bit. We don't want him getting agitated, causing more harm, so we're keeping him under mild sedation to give his body a little more time to adjust," she explained. "He'll be awake before you know it. I promise."

Knowing there was no chance of me leaving my father's side, Frankie sent Angus and Colin home, sending Gia along with them to rest. Carl and Audrina were back and forth, refusing to leave me alone for long. They'd also called Cynthia, my father's secretary, and filled her in on what had taken place. She arrived at the hospital almost immediately, working the entire time by issuing press releases, fending off reporters, and keeping the staff members up to date on my dad's progress. The press had already let it leak on the news that the Senator and his wife had been in an accident with a drunk driver, which resulted in deaths, but had withheld the names of the deceased until families had been notified. All of it had done little more than cause speculation and false reports, neither of which were needed right now.

After hours of sitting, Frankie excused himself to make a few phone calls. After a while, I decided to slip out to find him and get some fresh air myself. When I stepped outside, I saw Cynthia on her phone, and as our eyes met, she ended the call and headed directly toward me. She'd been with my father since he'd become a senator, keeping his life in order and sticking by his side always, but never in the limelight.

"Lexi," she said, clearing the distance. "I'm so sorry for your loss. I'm here to do anything I can to help you get through this," she said, pulling me into a tight hug before taking a step back and meeting my gaze, her own eyes glassy with emotion. "I very much respect and admire the man in that room."

"Thank you." I swallowed hard, my head swimming. "Right now, I just need him to wake up, so we can face this together. I have so many things to take care of, the first being I need to release my mother's body to the funeral home and start the arrangements," I managed. "I just don't want to do that until my father is awake. She was his wife, after all. He doesn't even know," I said, looking back at her in defeat. "I have no idea what to do. I feel like I'm on autopilot."

"I'll help you," she promised, squeezing my hand. "In the meantime, you need rest and food. You're not good to anyone if you make yourself sick."

Nodding in agreement, I looked up to find my knight in shining armor coming towards me with food and coffee.

"Baby? Are you okay?" he asked, glaring at Cynthia as if she were the enemy.

"Yes." I nodded, rubbing his arm in appreciation. "Frankie, this is my dad's secretary, Cynthia. Cynthia, this is my boyfriend, Frankie."

If I were not facing the biggest shit storm of my life, I would have laughed at her reaction.

""Um, hi," she stammered, trying desperately not to check him out as she extended her hand professionally. "It's a pleasure to finally meet you. Senator Cole has spoken highly of you."

"The pleasure is all mine," Frankie said, flashing the signature smile as he placed his arm on my shoulder and pulled me close. "Thank you for taking care of the senator's affairs so Lexi can focus on her dad."

"Of course." She nodded, facing me once more. "Lexi, honey, you call me with anything else you need, and I will get right on it. Right now, I will take care of the press. Don't worry about a thing. Please let me know when Jackson..." She cleared her throat, correcting herself as she nervously brushed her pants. "Senator Cole wakes."

"I will," I promised, returning her hug before watching her turn back down the hallway.

"Come on, babe. We need to get some food into you," he said, taking my hand and leading me toward the lounge. "I would take you out to the bench in the courtyard for some fresh air, but the press is swarming around out there. That's the last fuckin' thing you need to deal with right now."

With my nerves, it took all I had to force the food down and keep it there. We ate in silence, but once we were finished, Frankie had had enough of the quiet. He leaned into me, lifting my chin to bring my gaze to his.

"Lexi, honey, I know you're hurting." He sighed, searching my features. "Losing your mother is... fuck, it's got to be devastating." He shook his head. "I want to help you get through this, but you've got to let me in."

"I'm okay, Frankie," I said, looking at him. "I hope what I am about to say won't make you think differently of me. I'm ashamed to even say it out loud, but..." I swallowed hard, facing him. "If I'm being honest, a part of me feels like it's a relief that she's gone." Looking up at him, I waited for the disgust to cross his face, knowing no daughter should say things like this about her mother, but instead, I only found compassion. "Ever since I could remember, she was always making me feel worthless. I was never good enough. In public, she would pretend to be the doting mother, getting my hopes up, only to be dashed when we came home and were behind closed doors. I've tried so hard all my life, but it never mattered what I did, I just wasn't good enough," I whispered, thankful when he pulled me into his lap, holding me close. "I am sad that I couldn't be the daughter she wanted, but there's a part of me that's grateful I don't have to keep begging her to be loved."

"Baby, don't ever feel guilty about how you feel," he whispered into my hair, stroking my back affectionately. "I didn't know her well, but it seems to me she had her own demons and tried to make them yours. No child should ever have to endure that or have to fear their mother as you did yours," he continued. "You did the best you could. Don't ever doubt that."

His words touched my soul so deeply. I could do little more than nod my reply before he continued.

"You and your dad will need to talk when this all blows over. I mean no disrespect, but he needs to finally know the truth. You both owe it to yourselves now that she's gone. Maybe everyone can make amends."

After watching my father toss and turn most of the night, his brows furrowing every so often as though he was struggling,

I was exhausted. Sitting in the chair next to him, I rested my head on his hand as a small child would do looking for comfort from a parent. Frankie was sound asleep in the recliner.

It was late when my phone pinged with a text, startling me enough to cause me to jolt in my seat, the legs scraping the floor and making Frankie stir. Moving to the window for my phone, I felt my stomach drop when I saw a new text, relieved instantly when I saw it was Shelby.

> **Hey, sweetie. I know you are probably overwhelmed, but I just wanted you to know I will be there tomorrow. Gia and Colin are picking me up at the airport. I love you.**

> *Thanks. I wish you were coming here under different circumstances but knowing you and Gia are here will help me get through this nightmare. Love you. I'll see you tomorrow.*

Turning around, I slammed into Frankie's chest, gripping my own.

"Jesus, you scared me," I gasped, staring up at him. "Stalk much?"

"With you? Yes," he admitted bluntly. "I am scared you will not tell me shit for fear of worrying me, so if I have to sneak up on you? So be it," he said softly, brushing my hair away from my face. "I have your back. Don't ever question that," he whispered, placing a tiny kiss on the tip of my nose.

As I laid my head on his chest, inhaling his scent for the first time in two days, I felt like it was all going to be okay.

My father began to moan once again and immediately, I turned my attention to him and reached for his hand.

"Daddy, shhh. It's okay, stay still," I said, trying to remain calm as I watched his eyes slowly begin to flit open, squinting at the harsh light. "You're in the hospital. You've been in an accident."

Turning to look at me, his eyes still swollen and bruised, his lips cracked as they began to move slowly.

"Water," he croaked out, his voice shallow and broken. "Please."

I reached for the cup of water on the table nearby, retrieving the blue sponge soaking inside and began swiping it over his lips, offering him some relief. He closed his eyes, his tongue darting out to quench his thirst. In the next moment, we were surrounded by nurses, each of them checking an IV, bandage, and vitals.

"Good evening, Senator Cole." Amy smiled as she moved over him. "It's a pleasure to finally see those eyes open, sir," she said, patting his hand. She began to ask him a few simple questions. He tried to answer the best he could with his voice hoarse from dryness. "Once we're done, Senator, I will let the doctor know you are awake and he can come in and do his exam."

Stepping back, I felt Frankie's arms wrap around my waist as we watched my father do simple tasks like moving his toes and fingers, then his arms and legs. Although they were slow and unsteady, he was still able to move them, which gave me hope.

Finally letting out the breath I was holding, I was relieved, but scared knowing the next few hours were going to be the most difficult for both of us. Not only would he face his physical wounds, but eventually, he'd ask where my mother was, and I'd have no choice but to tell him.

Chapter Four

Lexi

Shortly after the doctor arrived, Frankie and I stood at the foot of the bed while we watched in silence.

When he finally spoke, it made my heart drop.

"Caroline..." he rasped as if it were all he could manage.

"Daddy, you need to rest," I said quietly, doing my best to avoid the inevitable. "We can talk later."

"No," he said, shaking his head in frustration as his eyes began to tear up. "Gone."

It wasn't a question. It was a statement.

As I found his eyes, I saw a storm of emotions. One look told me he knew the answer but needed me to validate his fears.

"Yes, Daddy," I said in a whisper, the tears falling over my cheeks as the words left my lips. "They tried to save her, but it was just too much," I managed, taking his hand as he reached for me, trying to comfort me as best he could, both of us crying for the loss of a mother, a wife. "She's gone, Daddy."

The days following were a nightmare, the press on us every minute trying to get an interview. Cynthia was a godsend, managing my father's affairs from his hospital room, releasing another press release, this time confirming my mother's death and asking for privacy. Somehow, everything else fell into place. It wasn't lost on me that it was due to her commitment to my father.

Once everything hit the media, it was bedlam. It was so severe that when we left the hospital to shower or eat, we went directly to Angus' house because the press was camped out at mine.

Since my father was in the hospital recovering and unable to attend, I planned my mother's funeral entirely with the help of my new family. The funeral director came to the hospital, helping us choose a casket, flowers and other elements of her service. They say when you're mourning, you experience seven different stages of grief. If that were true, my father was knee deep in pain, guilt, and depression, while I'd moved on to acceptance, knowing deep down, I wasn't sure what else to feel.

After a few phone calls, my father arranged for him and me to visit the funeral parlor alone to pay our respects privately as a family before the public. However, getting my dad out of the hospital safely and unnoticed was nothing short of a miracle. Thankfully, Angus came through for us once again, calling on a few of his club brothers to help with the escort and keep the press away.

Three of them arrived, each massive and intimidating, decked out in full leather with matching patches that read *Vipers: Charleston* across their backs. Rush, whose patch told me he was club president, was the first to introduce himself and also the most handsome. His blonde hair had flecks of grey that matched his goatee and made his steel blue eyes pop against his skin. His arms were comparable to tree trunks and his tattoos, like the rest of them, told his story.

His VP, Rusty, was next and the smallest of the three. He had jet-black hair and green eyes that reminded me of emeralds. He and Rush were both around my dad's age, while Cue, their Sergeant at Arms, seemed younger despite his bald head and black beard. The three of them filed in, greeting Angus with hugs and backslaps before speaking with my father, offering condolences as they shook his hand and waited for his nurses to get him ready to go. I learned immediately that these men commanded respect. I also learned that they gave it.

When we arrived at the funeral home, the overwhelming scent of flowers was intense as they brought us to the back entrance.

Her casket had been closed due to her injuries, knowing if she wasn't going to look perfect, she would come back to haunt me for sure. Instead, we placed a picture of her from the Red Cross gala, laughing, impeccably dressed in her silver gown, and wearing a smile that wasn't forced.

As I took in the room around us, I was overwhelmed by the number of tributes that had already started to arrive. It was the sharpest emotion sweeping over my anger. She spent all of her time with charities and social clubs, made so many friends in life, but couldn't show me an ounce of affection. When we reached her casket, my father motioned for Frankie and me to help him stand, grabbing him gently and lifting him slowly as he took a few shaky steps toward her. Placing his hand on top, he bowed his head.

"We may not have had the best of times, Caroline, but what we had together gave us a beautiful child. I hope you find the peace and forgiveness you desperately sought in this life and know that you were loved."

I knew even at that moment that his powerful words were something I would never forget.

When we got my father back to the hospital and settled, Cynthia was there, waiting. Knowing he wouldn't be alone, I decided that I needed to have a little girl time with Shelby and Gia at Angus' before meeting for dinner. On the drive over, I held Frankie's hand and savored in the way he smiled at me as I bent to kiss his knuckles.

"Are you ready for the next few days?" I asked, my eyes searching his face for any signs of fear.

"I am here for you Lexi. Through thick and thin, no matter what happens, I am not going anywhere," he promised. "Your life may be different than mine, but that's what makes us fit," he said, kissing my hand before pulling it into his lap. "We balance each other. No amount of press is going to scare me off."

When we pulled up to Angus', if I hadn't known better, I'd have thought he was throwing a party. Music was blaring from inside. Frankie and I puzzled as we stepped onto the back porch, finding Gia and Angus belting out their rendition of Bon Jovi's "Wanted Dead or Alive" while Shelby and Colin watched from the doorway, shaking their heads at them. Finally, when the final notes were over, they turned to us, Angus setting his mic to the side and facing me.

"Lexi, I hope you know we mean no disrespect, but we've all been walking around in a funk for the last few days," he offered as Gia and Shelby assaulted me with a group hug, squeezing me tight. "We need to cut loose. The best way to do that is some karaoke and good barbecue."

"It's okay." I smiled, turning my attention toward the girls.

"I have missed you so much," Shelby said, hugging me and shoving Gia out of the way.

"Give me some love, you twats," Gia insisted, pouting and crossing her arms like a little child.

Laughing for the first time in days, I knew that being here was the right choice.

"All right, you bunch of nuts," Colin said as he made his way down the steps. "Get the hell up here before you cause a scene."

"I'm hugging my friend," Gia snipped as he pulled her away, her aggravation doing nothing to move the smirk from his lips.

"Yeah, I got a hug for you, baby," he husked. "One you won't forget."

"Hug this, numbnuts." Gia rolled her eyes, sticking her tongue out and giving him the finger.

"All right." He shrugged. Without missing a beat, he lifted her over his shoulder, jogging up the steps as if she weighed nothing and giving her a sharp swat on the ass, her giggle trailing after them.

As Frankie took my hand, we followed everyone into the house, ready to have a little fun.

After dinner, we all sat on the patio, enjoying the summer night, the men sipping whiskey and talking business while us girls drank wine and caught up on things other than the funeral.

We'd covered just about everything when the nagging concern in the back of my mind finally wouldn't relent.

"Can I ask the two of you for a huge favor?" I started, hating what was coming despite their nodding replies. "Once this is all over, I'm going to have to go through all of her things. I'm not sure my father will be able to handle it." I sighed, shaking my head as I studied my wine glass. "Most will go to charity. It's what she'd have wanted. But even if I have little attachment to most of it, it's still going to be really hard for me. I don't think I can do it alone, either."

"Of course, Lexi," Shelby said, reaching for my hand. "Whatever you need, we will be right there for you. You know that."

"I can't even imagine losing my mom or Nonna," Gia said, hugging me close. "My heart breaks knowing you're going through this, that you didn't have a close relationship with her, but my family? We're here for you, Lex. No matter what."

We were lost in our moment when the guys joined us, Frankie leading them toward us as he smiled down at his phone.

"Ma will be here tomorrow," he said, pulling me close. "She got a nurse to stay with Nonna so that she could be here for you."

"I can pick her up from the airport," Angus offered, taking a sip from his whiskey as he grinned behind his glass. "Just let me know when she'll be ready for me."

"You keep your ass here and work, old man," Frankie objected, raising his eyebrows. "Lexi and I can pick her up."

"No problem." Angus grinned, raising his hands in surrender with a chuckle. "I'm just saying... she looks anything like that sister of yours, I'd be a fool to not at least introduce myself." He winked, pulling Gia in for a hug as Frankie growled.

"I don't care if you're old," he snipped. "I can still kick your ass, and don't you forget it."

"Okay, boys. That's enough. Put your peckers away and calm your asses down," Colin began, facing his father and pulling Gia under his arm. "You will act like a perfect gentleman when Mrs. Moretti arrives. And you?" he continued, turning toward Frankie. "You need to let your mother have a little fun instead of locking her up in a tower."

"Jesus Christ." Gia rolled her eyes. "I feel like a tennis ball being tossed back and forth."

"Oh, I'll bounce you around, baby." He smirked, kissing her hair. "Just say the word."

"Your father has a better shot of getting laid than you do."

"Well, I just threw up in my mouth a little," Frankie said, shaking his head before glancing toward me. "If you're ready, we're staying in the guest room tonight. You need to get some rest."

"Who is going to stay with my dad? I don't want to leave him alone."

"Already covered. Cynthia, Audrina, and Carl are taking shifts."

"Always thinking, aren't you, Mr. Moretti?"

"I've gotta be on my toes with you, baby." He winked, swatting me on the ass before gesturing toward the stairs. "Now get up there."

I made my way toward the room, grateful when the door was finally shut behind us. For the first time in days, we were alone. When it came to Frankie Moretti, I was beginning to find there was nowhere else I'd rather be.

After breakfast, the guys headed to the office while the girls and I lounged around, waiting until it was time to pick Theresa up from the airport. I checked in with my dad, happy that he seemed to be doing better.

The wake had been scheduled for later that afternoon, the burial the following morning. I'd be lying if I said I wasn't feeling completely overwhelmed. I sat alone on the back porch, trying my best to collect my thoughts and prepare for what I was about to experience.

It wasn't lost on me that my mother had devoted her life to charity rather than my father and me. That had always been one of the things that made me feel so insecure. At that moment, I made the decision that, once this was all behind me, I'd begin focusing on my own happiness for once.

My cell phone ringing pulled me from the thoughts, and when I looked down and saw it was Frankie, I answered with a smile, knowing his voice would calm me more than anything else could.

"Hey, you," I said, my voice breathy. "When are you coming to get me? I miss my man."

"Hey, sweetie. I should be there in about fifteen minutes to pick you up. Ma's flight comes in around ten thirty, so I thought if it was all right with you, we could get her checked in and settled at the hotel. When you're ready, we can pick her up, and she can ride with us tonight."

"You're not letting her stay here with us?" I asked, a bit surprised since there was plenty of room, and he'd offered more than once.

"No, I don't think it's a good idea," he said. "We've already taken over his house. I wouldn't feel right adding another person to that. Besides, it'll give my mom a little privacy, and she'll still be close enough if you need her."

"If you say so." I sighed, shrugging to myself. "I just think it's silly for her to stay all the way across town when the rest of us are already here."

"Well, I want to get you through the next few days, Lexi. I'd rather not spend it worrying about my mother getting hit on," he finally admitted, making me roll my eyes.

"Frankie, you can't be serious. Listen, I know you're protective of Gia and your mother, but Angus has been nothing but respectful as well as a good friend. Not only that, they've got a lot in common. They'd probably really enjoy each other's company," I insisted. "There's no sense in making her stay in a hotel. You're acting like a caveman right now. Just bring her here."

Frankie was silent for a moment before finally releasing a sigh of defeat.

"Fine," he huffed. "But Lexi, I swear to God, if he hits on her, I'm gonna lose my shit. It's bad enough I've got to deal with Colin chasing Gia around like a dog in heat. The last thing I need is Angus taking a run at my mother."

When I saw Theresa on the escalator, relief washed over me knowing she would be there for me during this challenging time. I had depended on her more in the past year than I ever had my own mother and was grateful to have her in my life. As she reached us, she wrapped her arms around me, holding me close as I fell apart right there in the middle of the airport. Once I was able to get a hold of my emotions, she released her grip on me, but moved her hand into mine, never letting go as we headed for our car.

"No hug for your only son, huh?" Frankie teased, leaning in with a playful pout as he kissed her cheek.

"Oh, hush, you." She swatted at him, pulling him close enough to miss him sticking his tongue out at me, making me smirk. "Come here and give your mother some love."

We made our way to the car, not yet out of the parking lot when Frankie began rubbing his face in frustration, reluctantly facing her. "There's been a slight change in plans."

"What's that?"

"Some of us thought," he started, as he cut his eyes at me in the rearview. "That it'd be better for you to stay with us at Angus McGrath's place instead of a hotel. If you're not comfortable with that, though—"

"Thank Christ!" she exclaimed with relief. "The thought of staying so far away from you kids was making me crazy," she admitted. "Besides, I can't wait to meet Angus. The girls have gone on and on about how handsome he is."

The wink she shot back to me wasn't nearly as amusing to Frankie.

"Ma, if he gets all up in your business, you've got to promise me you'll tell me," he insisted. "I'll kick his ass, friend or not."

"Frankie, I'm old enough to take care of myself." She waved him off as he pulled onto the interstate. "And I'm not dead, you know. It might be nice to get hit on every once in a while."

"Fuck my life…"

When we arrived at Angus', everyone was already there waiting for us. Gia and Shelby came running down the stairs, greeting her with hugs and kisses while Angus remained at the door, his arms crossed and an expressionless face as Colin welcomed her with a kiss on the cheek.

"Theresa," Colin said, gesturing to Angus as he led her up the steps toward him, Frankie following closely behind with her bag. "This grumpy old man is my father."

"Mr. McGrath." She nodded, her eyes locked on his immediately as she extended her hand. "Thank you for inviting me to stay in your home and taking such great care of my family."

"The pleasure is mine, Mrs. Moretti," he said, taking her hand gently before leading her inside. "Please, make yourself at home. You and your family are more than welcome." He glanced back at Colin. "Please show Theresa to her room and make sure she's settled," he continued, returning his eyes to hers. "If you'll excuse me, I've got a few things to attend to."

"Of course." She nodded, her eyes trailing after him as he quickly slipped down the hallway before they moved to Frankie. "Are you sure it's not a problem for me to stay here?"

"Not at all, Ma," he said, kissing her cheek. "Just some work stuff. He mentioned a deadline with Castagna earlier."

"Okay," she shrugged, turning toward me. "Lexi, what time will we be leaving for the services?"

"It begins at four."

"I'll just get changed and settled and will be back down to work on lunch. We can talk if you're up to it," she suggested, pulling a grateful nod from me. "Colin, would it be alright if I used the kitchen?"

"Absolutely," he beamed. "Work your magic."

"Brown-nose," Gia mumbled, rolling her eyes. "Okay, Ma. Let's get you unpacked."

Colin

While I might have been slowly beginning to melt the ice over Gia's heart, I had no idea what was going on with my father. I'd grown used to his loud and overbearing behavior, but the second Theresa arrived, he'd acted in ways I'd never seen from him before.

Once she was settled, and I was able to step away, I made my way downstairs to his study. I found him with his back facing the door and his eyes locked on a picture of my mother on the bookcase.

"Can I help you with something, son?" he asked as he glanced over his shoulder.

"Nope, just checking in," I said, moving further into the room. "You okay? You were pretty short with Theresa."

"Was I?" he asked, clearing his throat before finally turning toward me and shuffling through papers on his desk. "I'll be sure to apologize. I didn't mean to make anyone uncomfortable. I've just got a lot on my mind and want to take care of a few things so we can focus on everything here over the next few days."

"Okay." I shrugged. "I told her she could use the kitchen, so when you're ready, come join us for lunch."

He nodded, and I moved back toward the door, knowing there was much more to the story, but leaving it for now.

Chapter Five

Frankie

While Shelby and Gia helped my mother unpack, I thought Lexi could use some fresh air before we headed to the funeral home. It was apparent she was battling a million emotions. I remembered that feeling from when my dad died. I was seventeen and Gia was ten, both of us way too young to bury a parent. The memories of standing next to Ma and Nonna, trying to be the support system for them while we all stared at his casket, was hell on earth. I thought back then that if stayed in that room, he was with me and things would be okay, but the second I left, he'd be gone forever. No matter how hard I tried to block out our reality, his last words replayed in my mind.

I'd sent Ma for coffee, and it was just him and me. Despite his labored breathing, he grabbed my hand and met my eyes, his own moist with tears. *Son, I've fucked up plenty,* he said. *I'll make amends on the other side, but I'll always be watching over all of you. You just have to promise me to keep this family together, no matter how hard it might seem sometimes. You've got to keep them safe and close. When it comes time to leave, family's all you've got.*

Lost in the memory once again, my heart broke for Lexi, knowing she'd never had that with anyone but her father. As I glanced over at her, though, I knew I'd do all I could to make sure she did from now on.

"Come on, babe. Let's take a walk," I said, taking her hand and leading her outside.

"Okay, I could use some fresh air. My stomach is doing flips. I am starting to get nervous," Lexi, said biting her lip while looking to me to give her comfort.

The McGrath plantation had a beautiful meadow of green grass surrounded by trees that eventually led to the water. I found a spot beneath a massive oak tree with twisted limbs and sat at its base, helping her settle between my legs as I wrapped my arms around her, savoring the way she leaned into my chest. We sat quietly for a long while before finally, her soft voice broke the silence.

"Frankie?"

"Yeah, baby?"

"I wish my dad could be with me. I'm not sure I can do this on my own."

"I know you want your dad here, but that doesn't mean you'll be alone," I whispered, pressing my lips to the top of her head. "I'll be right there with you the whole time. You'll have your friends, your family... all of us are here, Lexi."

"Thanks," she managed, her voice breaking as she leaned back into me.

We sat together for a while, talking little and holding each other tight until her phone chimed. A quick look lifted our spirits as we read Gia's dramatic message.

Would you two please get your asses back here already? We are all starving. Ma won't cook until you're both back. I am about to eat my arm, for fuck sake.

"Come on," I said with a sigh as I stood, helping Lexi to her feet. "I've got your back today," I whispered, placing feathery kisses on her lips. "Every day, baby."

"Frankie, I don't know what I did to deserve you. I never thought I could love someone as much as I love you," she admitted, glancing up at me with teary eyes before pressing her lips to mine, giving me a deep kiss. "You make me so happy, my heart hurts."

"I feel the same way about you," I whispered, resting my forehead on hers, the feel of my dick swelling making me close my eyes before clearing my throat. "Okay, come on. I'm trying to be a decent guy, and you're making it very hard." I smirked at the double edge to my words.

"Fine, but don't think I won't remember you chose food over me." She shrugged, letting out a light giggle, the sound beautiful enough to have me lean in for another kiss before heading back to the house.

Lexi

We could hear the laughter trailing from the house before we made it to the door.

"What the fuck?" Frankie blurted as we rounded the corner to the kitchen.

Theresa was beside the counter, head tilted back with an Oreo over her eye, squishing her face slowly to edge the cookie closer to her mouth as the girls cheered her on. Colin was across from her, attempting the same feat but failing miserably.

We stood watching from the doorway until the Oreo made it close enough to retrieve with her tongue and claim victory. She shook her ass before kissing her competitor on the cheek sweetly.

"Reigning champ, Theresa Moretti," Shelby announced, reaching for Mama's arm and lifting it into the air while a shift from the corner pulled my eyes away to find Angus watching quietly.

Gia moved toward Colin, swiping her finger over his lip and sliding it into her mouth seductively.

"You're not playing fair, Gia," he groaned.

"I never do." She smirked.

"Hmm." He chuckled before abruptly tossing her over his shoulder and slapping her ass. "Neither do I."

As they slipped by us, laughter trailing up the stairs after them, Theresa began fanning herself with a smirk.

"I'm too old to be dancing around the kitchen like that." She chuckled.

"You're never too old, Mrs. Moretti," Angus said, breaking his silence from the corner. "We both know life is too short to not enjoy the little things."

"Please, Angus, call me Theresa," she said. "I feel old as dirt being called Mrs. Moretti."

Turning to look out the window, he whispered, "You're far from that, Theresa."

Theresa smiled and moved toward the fridge, her blush not lost on me as she pulled a few things out to make lunch.

"Lexi," she said, her voice sad. "I'm sorry, honey. I shouldn't be dancing around the kitchen like a fool while you're enduring such pain. I meant no disrespect."

"Don't. I grew up in a home without laughter. This was exactly what I needed."

Shelby

Although I wasn't looking forward to what the next few hours would bring, I couldn't deny my relief when it was time to retreat to my room to prepare for the service. I was happy my friends were happy. However, after losing your first love, knowing you'll never hold them again, it was getting to be a little much for me.

Seeing Gia and Lexi made me think of what I could've had if Drew were still here. They had no idea how lucky they were, no idea how hard it was to feel like you'd never be whole ever again after having to say goodbye to someone you cared for so deeply. Some days, I felt like I'd wander the earth forever just waiting to be reunited with Drew.

When I moved to Boston, I'd hoped it would be the first step in rebuilding myself when Montana became too painful. I'd hoped I'd find someone to make me feel that way again instead of the pity back home.

I hadn't told the girls about Drew. Right then, I wanted to keep it tucked deep down inside me. I was not ready to tell that story or open that wound just yet.

After the funeral, Gia and I would stay with Lexi and help her get her mother's affairs in order. Then, we'd head back to Boston before school started. I was ready to be back at the stables, keeping my mind busy and surrounding myself with all the things that brought me peace.

"Shelby, can I come in?" Gia called from the other side of the door.

"Sure, I'm not naked or anything." I smirked. "Not that it has ever stopped you before."

"Okay, good," she said, closing the door behind her and falling onto the bed with an exhausted sigh. "So, I'm fucked, and I need your help. I'm not sure what to do with Colin."

"What do you mean *do*?" I asked, taking a seat beside her.

"You know." She shrugged suggestively, pointing to her girly parts. "What do I do?"

"I can't tell you that." I chuckled. "That's between y'all. What does your heart say?"

"I don't know. I really like him, but I've been hurt so many times. I'm scared." She sighed. "I don't want to get fucked again. No pun intended."

"Well, if he gets his way, you will in at least one way." I chuckled. "Boys got it hard."

"In more ways than one." She winked, grinding her hips and making me laugh.

"You're nuts, Gia."

"Yeah," she agreed, growing quiet before we leaned back against the mattress, her eyes sad when she glanced over at me. "This afternoon is going to suck. I feel so bad for Lex."

"Me, too." I nodded, biting my lip in thought before looking back over at her. "You know, you and I are lucky enough to have such great families that losing anyone of them would be like taking a limb, but Lexi never had that relationship with her mother. Now that she's gone, she'll never know if they could have fixed it."

I moved my eyes toward the ceiling not wanting to make eye contact with her as my thoughts went back to Drew. When I lost him, it was like a piece of me died, and it wasn't long before I knew I'd never get that back. The reality of that made my eyes moist. It was a moment before I could face Gia again.

"You can see she is struggling with her emotions, not sure what to feel. She wants to mourn the loss of her mother, but that broad was so horrible to her. She's feeling guilty that she can't grieve as a child should. I would die a thousand deaths if that was Ma or Nonna. I can't even imagine."

"Well, that's why we are here," I said, finally looking at her again. "We'll just have to help her get through the rough patches."

"Yup, we got her back," she agreed, sticking her pinky out for me to wrap mine around, neither of us breaking the link as we rested our arms on the bed between us.

For a moment, we fell silent, the gravity of what was coming hitting us both as we considered what this would mean for our friend.

"So, speaking of backs," I finally said, elbowing her. "Are you going to lie on yours for Colin?"

"Oh, my God. You're such a bitch." She laughed, yanking the pillow out from behind me and smacking me hard. "I'm never talking to you again."

Lexi

As I stared back at my reflection, the bags beneath my eyes more prominent against my unusually pale skin, I cringed. Even if I hadn't felt it in my body between caring for my father and preparing for the next two days, one look and it was apparent. *My mother would shit a brick if she saw how I looked right now*, I thought to myself, swallowing hard as I gave myself a final once-over.

I'd chosen a classic black, knee-length dress and pulled my hair back in a chignon. Despite the emotion coursing through me, I knew I needed to be presentable. I was, after all, Alexis Cole—a perfect daughter. Even after her death, I was still desperate to please her.

I released the deep sigh in my chest, glancing down at the pearls that had been hers. As a child, I longed to play with her. Now that I was burying her, I simply longed to be worthy. I thought it would be nice to wear a piece of her today, but now that it was time, the thought of doing so filled me with guilt.

"You look beautiful," Frankie whispered as he kissed my cheek, the feel of his palms moving up my arms pulling my eyes back to the mirror to study his reflection. "How are you holding up, baby?"

"I'm okay," I said, unsure if it was honest or not. "You look very handsome," I said, grateful I knew the truth in that.

He was wearing a black Ralph Lauren suit with a matching tie, the crisp white of the shirt bright against his olive skin.

"Thank you," Frankie said, giving me a small smile in return as he continued staring at me in the mirror. "Are you almost ready?"

"As I'll ever be."

"Do you want me to help you with that?" he gestured toward the pearls I was still clinging to. My eyes remained locked on the necklace until the sound of my phone distracted me from him.

"It's my dad," I said quietly, putting the phone to my ear. "Hi, Daddy. Are you alright?"

"Yes, I just wanted to call you before you left," he replied, his voice still weak. "Lexi, I'm so sorry I can't be there with you today. You've grown into such a strong woman, but no child should ever have to bury their parent alone."

"It's okay," I whispered, his words making my voice thick. "Daddy, I know you'd be here with me if you could. Just promise me you'll focus on getting better so you can come home."

"I promise, sweetie," he said softly, his voice growing silent for a long moment before he cleared his voice and finally broke the silence. "And I couldn't ask for a better man to stand with you today. Please thank Frankie and his family as well as the McGraths. I am blessed to have such wonderful people around you."

"I will. Daddy, can I ask you something?"

"Of course."

"Once this is all behind us, can we talk?"

"You can always talk to me, Lexi," he offered. "We can talk right now, honey."

"I just wanted to know if she ever said anything..." I trailed off, my voice choking with emotion. "Daddy, I can't live the rest of my life wondering what I could have done differently to make her love me."

"It wasn't you, honey," he started. "Lexi, I'll never forget your mother. She gave me the most precious gift of my life when she gave me you, but there were things..." he whispered, his voice fading out for a moment. "Once we're past this, once I'm healed, I promise we'll talk more, but don't ever think you're not loved. I love you more than anything."

"I love you, too," I said gently, wiping my cheeks. "I have to go now, but I'll come and see you once we're finished."

We hung up, and I turned to walk out, finding Frankie leaning against the frame of the door, watching me.

"I'm so proud of how strong you've been through all of this," he began, his eyes locked on mine as he cleared the distance between us. "Today will suck, but I promise if you need anything, I'm here for you, baby."

"Thank you," I whispered, giving him a quick kiss.

It was time for me to be the daughter I was raised to be.

When we pulled up to the funeral home, it seemed Angus had once again called upon the Vipers to help my family by having them create a human shield built of leather and muscle to keep the press at bay. Despite the mass of photographers and news teams eager to intrude, musclebound men and chrome were all that could be seen.

On the steps stood the three men I'd met in the hospital, Rush, Rusty and Cue. When I opened my door, I was met by yet another handsome biker who introduced himself as Rooster. He helped me from the car first before attending to Theresa and Audrina and then signaled with his arm to four others who joined him immediately.

"Ma'am, on behalf of the Charleston Vipers, please accept our deepest sympathy for your loss," Rooster said. "The senator has supported many of our charity runs, and we are here to make sure you and your family get inside safely. Please stay close to my men."

Nodding my head in awe, Frankie, Colin, Angus, and Carl joined them, forming a circle around the women as we were escorted into the building.

"Holy shit, Lexi," Gia whispered, her voice loud enough for Angus to hear. "Who the hell are these guys?"

"This is my club," Angus said. "When my wife was diagnosed, I retired to help care for her and Colin, but occasionally, I still call on them when I need help," he explained, glancing at Theresa for a moment, presumably to gauge her reaction. "That's what you do with family."

"I think it's wonderful these men have your back." Theresa smiled, patting Rooster's arm.

"Lexi, the press and photographers are like a swarm of locusts," Shelby said, grabbing my hand. "No wonder you hid at Colin's house."

"I am used to it Shelby, but today is not a day I would like captured in a photograph."

Reaching the top step, Rush, Rusty, and Cue formed a barricade. When I saw Mikey and Joey make their way from the top of the stairs, I began to cry as they pulled me in for a hug. At that moment, I realized this was the type of loyalty and love I had been searching for.

Once inside, the smell of the flowers hit me. They were lining the walls and overflowing into the adjoining rooms. I was amazed at the amount there, but then again it was my mother. She cared for many things; I just didn't happen to be one of them.

When I made it to the doorway, I froze in place, simply taking in the mahogany box in the center of the room. As my breathing began to quicken, I felt Theresa's arms wrap around me, hugging me close.

"Would you like to be alone, honey?"

"I don't know," I admitted, embarrassed as I looked up at her. "I'm not sure what I'm supposed to do."

"Lexi, remember. We're all here for you," Frankie said, kissing my temple from his place on the other side of me. "You don't have to do any of this alone."

"She never listened to me in life," I whispered, my voice closing with emotion as my eyes stayed locked on the casket. "Why would death be any different?"

"Honey, why don't you take some time alone?" Theresa suggested. "Say your peace so you can be free of all those feelings."

"Okay." I nodded before they both left the room, leaving me with her.

I gave myself a moment, collecting my nerves before I braved the few steps that would take me to the padded bench beside her. I swallowed hard as my eyes ran over the smooth wood before finally, I bowed my head, willing her to listen.

"I tried," I whispered, clenching my eyes tight, desperate to stop but knowing this was something I needed to do for us both. "My entire life was devoted to trying to please you, make you proud, but it wasn't enough. I simply lost who I was along the way." The tears finally came, and with them, I found the strength to push on and say the words I'd swallowed so many times before. "There was a time I gave so much to you, I felt as though a piece of me had been stolen. I never knew the look of a mother's love, only her disappointment. You made me feel cheated. Why was it so hard for you to love me? Why was I never good enough for you?" I whispered, shaking my head. "I'd hoped someday I'd have those answers, but now it's too late, so I simply hope that someday, you find peace. I may not have been good enough for you in this life, but I love you enough to hope you find that in the next."

Finally, I opened my eyes, the emotion in my throat so thick that I felt sick as my shoulders continued to shake from the sob slipping from my chest. I stood, grateful for the strong hand that was there to help steady me before drying my tears.

As I released a deep breath, one that felt like it had been lodged in my chest for the entirety of my twenty years, I blew it out and with it left the weight that had always resided on my shoulders.

"Are you ready?" Frankie whispered, pressing his lips to my temple as I gave him a nod. "Okay. Come on, baby."

I hesitated for a moment, burning this memory into my mind for safe keeping before I kissed my palm and pressed it to the cold wood, letting her go.

After greeting the sea of people and politicians who came to pay their respects, I was exhausted.

Frankie never wavered beside me. Whether it was taking care of my every need or just holding my hand to show his support, he stood by my side without fail, just as he'd promised. If it hadn't been clear before that day, it certainly was at the end of it that this man was mine for a reason, and I'd be a fool not to cherish him for the rest of my life, regardless of what was to come.

The next day I was in awe at the procession of motorcycles and cars that followed our limo. She would have been mortified with the Vipers and what they represented. However, she was blind to the fact they were great men whom I would always treasure.

I drifted in and out of my thoughts during the service, catching only bits and pieces of what the priest was saying. The faces surrounding me were a blur until I came upon Angus, Colin, Mikey, and Joey who stood with their hands folded in front of them, heads bowed in respect. I knew without even turning around that my two best friends were directly behind me in support of my loss. They never left my side, not even for a minute. I thanked God each day for bringing them into my life.

Frankie took my hand and motioned for me to place my rose on the casket before the others paid their respects. His unwavering grip on me offered the strength I needed to get through that moment.

Knowing this would be the last time I would ever be with her, I kissed my palm and placed it on the cold, wet wood.

"May your soul finally rest in peace," I whispered and dropped the rose into the darkness, watching it settle against the concrete slab where she would remain for eternity.

I slipped from our bedroom, quietly making my way downstairs. Hot tea in hand as I settled onto Angus' porch, the roll of the early morning fog gave me the clarity I needed to prepare for the day ahead

My heart was heavy. Not only had I just lost my mother, but Frankie, Theresa and the boys would be leaving to head back to Boston in only a few short hours. I knew Frankie had work to catch up on, and his mother had Nonna to look after, but it didn't mean I wouldn't miss them.

"Lexi?" Theresa called gently from the door, stepping out to affectionately pat my shoulder before kissing my hair and taking the seat beside mine. "I wish I didn't have to leave you today, honey. I hope you know that I'm only a phone call away if you need me."

"I know," I smiled. "Thank you. My father should be released in a couple of days, and we've found a private nurse to stay with him, Audrina, and Carl. I'll have to go through her things." I sighed. "I know we just buried her and I should wait out of respect, but I don't want my father to have to deal with that. He needs to focus on getting stronger."

"The girls will help you with whatever you need to be done," she promised. "The best advice I can give you is to try and move past the negative. She wasn't perfect. I know you two had your demons, but despite that, she did amazing things for a lot of people. God willing, you'll have a daughter of your own someday. Don't damage her legacy. It's something you'll want to pass on to them," she continued, squeezing my hand. "It's what I always told Gia after her father died. In a world that is sometimes black and white, stand out. Be colorful and forgive."

Theresa was right. I could hate my mother and make her out to be a villain, blaming my failures on her, but I needed to stop the cycle, rise above it all, and be a better person. Caroline

Cole's legacy for helping people was extraordinary, and she should be remembered for her work.

Hearing the French doors close behind us, we both turned around to see Angus, hair a mess and shirtless with a pair of pajama bottoms hanging from his hips. He didn't see us around the corner as he walked out towards the edge of the grass drinking his coffee and scrubbing his face awake, oblivious as both of us stared at his beauty.

"Good Lord, child," Theresa said, fanning herself. Angus may have been in his fifties, but he was ripped, every inch of his body proof he didn't miss a day at the gym. "Those tattoos are work of art."

"Uh... yeah," I agreed, unable to move my eyes from him, either.

"He is a wonderful man with so much love to give, but he is lost in his wife's memory," she said, looking away in disappointment as she sipped her coffee. "He'll never see the beauty of another woman's love again."

Before she could say more, Angus' rugged voice slipped out, his eyes locked on the sky like he talked with it daily.

"I need your guidance, Mia," he said low. "My heart says no, but my mind is telling me yes. I need you to give me a sign, tell me it's time."

His eyes closed gently, silence filling the porch for a brief moment before he opened them in time to watch the red cardinal land on the birdfeeder just in front of him.

When he turned around a moment later, he finally noticed us.

"I'm sorry, ladies," he cleared his throat, setting his cup on the table. "I didn't know you were here. I'll get dressed."

We watched him as he went in, my eyes turning to find Theresa's still locked on the door.

"Are you okay?" I asked, my lips quirked up on either side. "Your face is beet red."

"Hot flash, honey," she said, billowing her shirt to ease the crimson. "Just a hot flash."

Shortly after, Angus came back out with a tray holding coffee and muffins, fully dressed, much to our disappointment.

"My apologies, ladies. The housekeeper is off for the day, so we'll have to make do with what I could find at the bakery," he said, placing the tray between us. "Theresa, it was wonderful having you here. I hope, considering everything, you've enjoyed your stay."

"I have. Hopefully, once my mother is stronger, I can come back and see more of it." She smiled, popping a piece of muffin into her mouth, moaning at the taste. "These are to die for."

"Well, when you do, you are always welcome to stay here. I would love to be your tour guide, only asking for a homemade meal in return. You are quite the cook." He chuckled. "Your son and I have a great business between here and Boston. I'll be traveling that way soon. Hopefully, you can return the favor by showing me around," he continued. "That boy of yours is a good kid. I know you must be proud of him for all he's accomplished at his age. Owner of such a lucrative construction company so young is almost unheard of."

His innocent compliment had me choking on my coffee, glancing at Theresa in panic as I searched for any conversation that would take attention from her finding out about Frankie's position at the company. She still had no idea he was the owner of Castagna.

"Angus, do you know if anyone has bought the old inn down on Church Street yet?"

"No," he said, his expression wild enough at my outburst to make me feel like I'd grown ten heads. "I believe there are tax liens on it and red tape holding it up."

"That's a shame," I said, my words coming out in haste as I struggled to squash Angus' slip of the tongue. "It would make such a beautiful inn again. I hate to see it sold and the owners not use it for what it was meant for."

I didn't miss Theresa's eyes moving back and forth between us suspiciously. I was about to say more about the inn, anything really to divert the conversation, but before I could, her voice filled the porch.

"Thank you, Angus," she said quietly. "When my husband died, Frankie really stepped up as the man of the house. He's made me proud in many ways. I'm very grateful for Castagna and all they've done for him and my family. I thank God every day for blessing me with two wonderful children."

The confusion on Angus' face as he turned to me was short-lived as he took in my wide eyes, begging him to drop it. Before any more damage was done, the door swung open, revealing the entire crew as they made their way out to the porch, thankfully squashing the subject for good.

Chapter Six

Frankie

When I kissed Lexi goodbye at the airport, I was grateful to know being away from her for long periods of time would not happen again. Since the winters were so unpredictable in New England, business was getting crazy with everyone wanting their construction sites shored up before the first snow started to fall.

"Bye, Ma," Gia said, giving her a hug. "Give Nonna a kiss for me."

"Theresa, thank you so much for being here," Lexi added, kissing her cheek. "I can't thank you enough for all you have done."

"Have a safe flight, Mama T," Shelby said, pulling her close for a hug of her own. "I can't wait to get back to Boston and spend some time with Nonna and you."

"I love you, girls," she said, returning their affections. "Take care of Lexi and help Angus and Colin out where you can."

Joey and Mikey were next, hugging the girls one by one. They began walking away before Mikey glanced over his shoulder toward Colin, his eyes narrowed in warning.

"Don't forget what I said," he spat. "Partner or not, you hurt Gia, I'm on the next plane to kick the shit out of you, *pretty boy*."

"Dude, have you met Gia?" Colin laughed, rolling his eyes. "Trust me. Anyone gets hurt in this situation, it won't be her. Calm your ass down and stop worrying about us. We're good."

Colin extended his hand in truce. It was apparent Mikey wasn't sure he wanted it as he stared down at him for a second, finally grabbing his hand with hesitance.

"Come on, tough guy," Joey said, shoving Mikey toward the counter. "Let's get going before we miss our flight."

"Come here, you," I said, pulling Lexi close and holding her tight. "I hope when you get home, you're ready to take care of your man," I whispered into her ear. "I don't think I can take sleeping in that big bed alone for long. Hurry back, baby."

She released a shiver as her lips found mine, my dick swelling between us.

"I'll miss you, too," she promised, making a sign over her heart. "And don't you worry. We'll make up for lost time."

With a wink, she turned me toward the counter and smacked me hard on my ass, shoving me toward my laughing mother.

"You're gonna pay for that later," I warned playfully.

"Looking forward to it."

Lexi

The girls and I promised we would help Colin and Angus catch up on paperwork and filing in the office while we were all here, so for the first couple of days I avoided my own stuff and worked. My father was being released from the hospital, and he would need my help at home. Thank God for yet another distraction that kept me from dealing with my mother's things. Cynthia had arranged everything for my father at the house, and because he was so stubborn, he was working from his hospital bed, making sure he didn't fall behind on his commitments to the people and our state.

I was sitting at Angus' desk reviewing an order when my phone began to ring, the number not one I recognized. With some hesitance, I swiped the screen and held it to my ear.

"Hello?"

After a brief pause, I heard his voice.

"Alexis, do not hang up," Craig said, his words coming out in a rush as I froze in place. "I know you don't want to talk to me, but I wanted to extend my deepest sympathy on the loss of your mother. I wanted to come but thought a call would be better considering..." he trailed off, clearing his throat. "If my family or I can do anything, please let us know."

"Thank you, Craig," I managed, my voice cold and calculated as I spoke. "I appreciate your call. I know my mother shared a special friendship with you and your family. My father and I also appreciate you not coming here. I think we both know that would have done nothing more than cause problems, but we appreciate you keeping her in your thoughts."

"Did you say, Craig?" Gia stormed in, moving toward the phone. "Give me the phone. If he's giving you shit or fucking with your head, I swear to God, I'll send Frankie over there to kick his ass right now."

Waving her away like a fly, I waited for Craig's response.

"Oh, is that Gia I hear?" Craig asked with disdain in his voice. "That's too bad. I'd hoped you'd taken your mother's advice and gotten rid of her and that riff-raff she calls a family."

"Honestly, Craig, I couldn't give two shits what you think of my friends or me. That 'riff-raff' has stuck beside me in ways you will never understand, so instead of giving you the anger I know you're hoping for, all you'll have is my pity. You'll never understand what it's like to have people give a shit about you because you're nothing more than a selfish prick. Thanks again for the call. Goodbye," I snapped, hanging the phone up and dropping it dismissively onto the desk in front of me.

"Oh, my—" Shelby started.

"What did that fucker just call me?" Gia cut her off, the exchange pulling my eyes to find them watching, mouths hung open in shock.

"Are you serious, Gia?" Shelby exclaimed. "She just told his sorry ass off, and all you heard was an insult to you?"

"Yeah, I'll show him riff-raff." She shook her head. "Next time I see him, I'm gonna punch him in the fuckin' throat."

"Who got your ass in a knot, baby?" Colin said from the doorway, gesturing for Gia to come closer. "Come here. I'll make it all better."

"Oh, shut up." She swatted at him. "I'm fine. Lexi just got a call from Craig trying to express sympathy for her mother, and he heard me in the background, so he called me riff-raff."

She rolled her eyes. "Lexi called him a prick and hung up on him."

"Well, if he calls back, give me the phone," he said, giving her a quick kiss. "I'll handle that piece of shit."

As our tough girl pulled away, her eyes stayed dreamy, drawing laughter from Shelby and me.

"I'm pretty sure he got the hint," I offered. "I need to get to the hospital. My father will need help getting settled once he's home this afternoon."

"Should we come with you or stay here and work?" Shelby asked.

"No, stay here. It's fine. Cynthia will be there to help me."

"Ladies, I think it's a good time to break for lunch," Angus suggested as he stepped inside with more files and paperwork. "My treat."

"Jesus, Angus! What the hell?" Gia started, helping him put everything down. "Is this shit multiplying?"

"Sorry, angel," he said with a sigh as he took in the stacks covering the desk. "It's been on my desk at home, and with everything going on, I totally forgot to bring it here," he explained, giving her apologetic, puppy eyes. "Do you forgive me?"

"Of course. You forget I work with my brother and his band of merry assholes." She waved him off with a shrug. "I'm used to dealing with stuff like this, but I'll expect lunch to be at that fancy ass restaurant." She raised her brow playfully before kissing his cheek. "It's the least you could do for working our fingers to the bone."

"Girl, if I were twenty years younger, I would give my son a run for his money." He chuckled. "Go grab your shit and let's go."

Shelby

I decided last-minute to stay behind and get a jumpstart on the new files, getting plenty done without distraction. I loved them all to death, but between Colin trying to maul Gia every ten minutes and the never-ending calls Lexi got from Frankie, it was impossible to get anything done. I thought working with my family was hard, but these people were so unorganized it was no wonder they couldn't find anything. Now that I had a little downtime, I wanted to do some exploring. After eating lunch in a beautiful park surrounded by oak trees, I took a walk downtown where I came upon a beautiful old church with three sets of stairs and massive wooden doors leading in. Eager to pay my respects, I went inside.

The smell of extinguished candles lingered in the air. The stained glass was spectacular, the sun shining through them casting a rainbow of light across the floor. Sitting in my pew, I took a moment to reflect on all the good in my life and thank whoever is responsible for bringing this greatness to me. I also took this moment closed my eyes and talk to Drew, asking him for guidance.

For the last year, I had done a great job hiding what was going on inside my head and heart from everyone, but I missed him so much, some days I could barely breathe. They say when you die, you come back to help those who need it the most. I needed Drew. I needed him to help me heal, to keep his promise of a lifetime of kisses, smiles and love. All I had now was a broken heart, tears and loneliness. Losing him left me with no hope, afraid to love again. I needed a sign that someday I could be happy.

A commotion behind the altar pulled my eyes open. A man was carrying a ladder, wearing earbuds and singing, "God Gave Me You," by Blake Shelton, so out of key, it sounded like he was in pain. It was obvious he had no idea I was there as he continued to sing, setting up his ladder to change a blub. He was very handsome. His blonde hair and muscular build made it hard to take my eyes away.

I stood up, my movements from the pew making him realize he wasn't alone as he spun to face me, giving me the first glimpse of his blue eyes, broad chest and tattooed arms that lay hidden beneath his t-shirt.

"I'm sorry," he said quickly, his voice raspy as he collected his ladder and began to leave. "I didn't mean to interrupt your prayer."

"You didn't." I shook my head, wringing my hands nervously. "I was finished and... well, really I just wanted to come inside and see the building while I enjoyed some quiet."

"Well, then you have come to the right place, ma'am," he said, propping the ladder against the wall beside him before taking a step closer. "This is one of the oldest churches in Charleston," he continued, looking around at the structure. "It's been here since 1891, still has all the original pews and altar. It's full of history," he said with such pride, you'd think he built it with his own two hands. "Aside from some weather damage to the steeple a few years back, this old girl is still intact."

"Are you the pastor?" I said, hoping he'd keep talking.

"Me? No. I am just the handyman around here. I own a small business and specialize in custom woodworking and renovation," he explained, leaning against the pew beside me. "Do you live nearby?"

"No." I shook my head. "My college roommate lives here. I'm just visiting her for a few days."

"Well, I hope you have time to enjoy our city while you're here." He smiled, extending his hand. "I'm Jake Montgomery."

"Hi, Jake," I smiled, taking his hand and loving the feel of the calluses that lay across his palm. "My name is Shelby Lansing. It's a pleasure to meet you."

"Well, Shelby it was a pleasure meeting you," he said, glancing down at his watch. "I'd love to stay and chat, but I'm late for a lunch date with my girl, so I'll wish you a good day."

"You, too." I smiled, swallowing my disappointment as I watched him collect his things. *Great, he's got a girlfriend, and I'm flirting with him in church.* "I'm actually heading out, too. It was nice to meet you, Jake."

I stepped into the sunshine, enjoying the warmth on my face before shaking my head at the sky, admonishing Drew.

"Smart ass," I whispered.

I walked back to the office and did my best not to think about Jake Montgomery. Along the way, I passed an old building, sad to find it falling apart, the landscape overgrown. The place must have been breathtaking back in the day. It had character, grace, and like all of us just needed a little love. I took a quick picture of it on my phone, eager to ask Lexi if she knew anything about it before I continued my journey back to the office. I walked in to find Gia sitting behind the desk and facing Colin, listening intently to whatever he was saying. When he heard me come in, he glanced over his shoulder and gave me a polite smile before facing her again.

"We'll finish talking over dinner, sweetie," he promised, leaning down to give her a kiss. "I have to go check on things in the yard, but I'll be back in a little while."

"Okay," she smiled, watching him go before moving to my temporary desk and taking a seat. "Where the heck did you go? I called your cell, and you didn't answer. I was about to send Angus out looking for you."

"Sorry, I had lunch in the park and on the way back, I saw a church that caught my eye, so I stopped," I said, not willing to get into a conversation about the man I met inside.

"Well, next time answer your friggin' phone, will you? This isn't Montana. You can't trust anyone in a different city, Wrangler Jane. Capisci?" She hopped down, heading back toward her side of the room when her steps slowed, and her eyes locked on something outside. "Mother of God, Shelby. You should see the guy Colin's talking to out in the yard. He is drop dead gorgeous. That wife of his is one lucky son of a bitch. Cute kid. They must put something in the water down here." She shook her head, retreating to her desk. "All right, back to work. This payroll ain't gonna do itself."

The phone rang, I reached for it, grateful for another distraction as I wrote down the rush order coming in over the line, not bothering to look up when I heard footsteps coming inside.

"Excuse me?" A sweet voice came from the edge of my desk, and I raised my eyes to find a beautiful little girl wiggling around nervously in front of me. "May I please use your bathroom?"

"Of course, sweetie." I smiled, my hand over the receiver. "Miss Gia will show you. It's right over there."

I finished the call and hung up the phone, finalizing the order when I heard talking just beyond the entrance.

"Thanks again, Colin. I appreciate you getting this stuff for me so quickly. That house I'm working on is pretty dated, and I'll need whatever you can throw at me to finish the job."

Colin's large frame blocked my view of the owner of the rugged voice, and I turned my attention back to the new file I was working on. Gia's and the little girl's exchange making me smile.

"Do you need any help?"

"Nope, I am a big girl and can do it all myself," she proclaimed, closing the door in Gia's face.

"Well, okay then." Gia chuckled, shrugging as she returned to her desk.

"So, we meet again," the voice said, closer this time. When I glanced up, I felt my jaw go slack. "Hello, Shelby Lansing."

Drew, I thought as I took in Jake Montgomery on the other side of my desk, *I'm kicking your ass when I get up there.*

"Hi Jake," I said, standing quickly and almost knocking my water over. "Nice to see you again."

"What the hell? How do you two know each other?" Gia asked as she approached us.

"Divine intervention." Jake winked, making my cheeks heat as he faced me.

"Well, I'm her roommate, Gia," she said, shaking his hand. "Pleasure to meet you."

"Hi, G—" he started, stopping abruptly as he stared back at her. "Wait, *Gia*? *Boston* Gia? The same Gia Colin talks about at poker until our ears bleed every week Gia?"

"The one and only," she said, her cocky smile growing wide.

"Yes, Jake," Colin said, resting his arm on her shoulders, marking his territory. "This is Gia. Stop flirting with her, or more than your ears will bleed."

"Oh, relax. I just didn't know she was visiting," he chuckled before glancing at me. "So, this is the roommate you were talking about? I thought you said she was from around here, but you weren't?" I was about to answer when his eyes went wide, and he began searching the room frantically. "Oh, shit! Where is Campbelle?"

"Bathroom," I answered him, gesturing toward the door.

"Oh, thank God," he said, gripping his chest. "She usually doesn't leave my side. She's very shy," he explained, making his way toward the door and tapping gently. "Campbelle? Honey? You okay in there?"

"Yes, Daddy," she answered. "I'm sorry. I couldn't hold it."

"Okay." He smiled. "Wash your hands."

"Okay!" she called back out, her voice so sweet we couldn't help but laugh at her.

A moment later, the door swung open and she scurried out, pushing her blonde ringlets away from her face.

"I'm done, Daddy," she said, giggling as he scooped her up and grabbing his face with her little hands, whispering into his ear.

"Well, sweetie, Mr. Angus isn't here right now. That's why there is no candy out for you to take."

"I have candy!" I said, louder than needed and drawing attention to myself.

"Where?" Gia asked, suspicious.

"I hid it in my desk because *some* people eat it all," I explained, making myself look like an even bigger loser.

"That's not awkward." Gia snorted, making me roll my eyes before smiling at Campbelle, holding out for her the jar that held my stash.

"Daddy, may I have a piece, please?" she asked, giving him her best puppy dog eyes.

"I guess one piece won't hurt." He smiled, setting her on the top of my desk where she looked in the jar, tapping her chin making sure the one she picked was the best. Finally making her choice, she opened the wrapper carefully and popped the candy in her mouth.

"Campbelle, what do you say, honey?"

"Thank you, ma'am."

"Aww." I smiled at her. "You're welcome Campbelle. I love those, too."

"Well, Shelby, it was great to see you twice in one day. How long are you here in Charleston?"

"I'll be heading back to school in Boston in about a week or so."

"Really?" he asked, his eyes lighting up slightly. "Well, maybe I'll see you again before you have to go. Third time's a charm."

Taken aback at how he could flirt with a perfect stranger while he had someone at home waiting for him, I swallowed my annoyed thoughts and returned to my desk. Some men were pigs.

"Thank you, but I doubt it," I said, my voice short with the offense he'd caused. "I am pretty busy."

Rapping his knuckles on my desk, he stared down at me for a second before he gave me a smile.

"Okay, well if you change your mind or have time, Colin here has my number."

Nodding my head and giving him a smile, I went back to work.

Colin and Jake were barely outside before Gia was at my desk with a thousand questions.

"Okay, spill," she said, sliding her chair over and planting her chin into her palm, waiting impatiently for me to talk. "There is no way in hell are you leaving here without giving me all the details on how you met that fine piece of meat. And don't leave anything out, either. You hear me?"

I set my pen down and leaned back in my chair, giving her every detail of our encounter in the church. Once the story was over, I gave her a shrug.

"That's it. It was nothing special, and even if it were, the guy's married with a kid. Even if I had it in me to be some side hussy, the whole thing sounds like a disaster waiting to happen."

"Hmm, you were right," she said. "That story was pretty boring, Shelbs." She smirked. "But he's married, off-limits, and gross for even trying to talk to you. You have to admit, though." She winked. "That's one hot *daddy*."

"Eww." I made a face, pushing her away from my desk. "Go back over there and get shit done, would you?"

"Fine, but I'm making it my mission to get you laid," she announced. "Operation: dust the cooter is now in full swing."

"Why don't you worry about your own dusty cooter?"

Lexi

Once my father was finally home and settled in, I was happy to see he was doing better than I'd thought he would be after his surgery. Cynthia was nearby to make sure he didn't overdo it, and the nurse would begin her visits the next morning, also helping to care for him. Audrina and Carl were just happy he was home. After years of being run ragged by my mother, an empty house had made them feel lost.

Once Cynthia took her leave for the day, and he'd had time to rest, I tapped gently on his door, surprised to find him standing beside the window with his cane. "Come on in," he said.

"Hi, Daddy. It's time for your pain medication," I said, walking closer with the pills and glass of water I'd brought him.

"Thank you, baby girl," he said, walking slowly to a chair beside the fireplace and taking a seat. "Please sit. I missed you."

"Are you sure you don't want to lay back down and rest?" I offered. "I don't want you to overdo it."

"No, baby girl, I am fine. I need to build my strength and lying in that bed is not helping me."

He stared at me for a moment when I noticed tears forming in his eyes. Not sure what to do I just took his hand and gave it a squeeze.

"Are you okay?" I asked.

"Yes," he said, his smile weak as he squeezed my hand in return, clearing his throat. "Lexi, I'm not sure if now is the best time, but I think it's important that we talk, clear the air," he started. "If you have any questions along the way, I'll do whatever I can to answer them. Before I begin, though, I need you to promise me that you'll keep an open mind and not judge anyone, okay?"

I swallowed hard, the fairytale ending I'd always dreamed of slowly drifting away with what he was about to tell me.

"Of course, Daddy."

Waiting for my father to gather his composure was torture. I could see the tears welling up in his eyes, and I didn't know what to do, so I sat silently and waited.

"Lexi," he started, his face going flush for a moment as he searched for composure—something I'd never seen him do before, and I prayed I'd never see again. Despite the fact I wanted nothing more than to comfort him, I didn't know how, so I just waited. Eventually, he was ready. "Honey, I don't know where to start, so I am just going to start at the very beginning, so you have the entire story."

"Okay," I whispered.

"Your mother and I were college sweethearts. We came from similar backgrounds, and that was what drew us together," he began. "Both of us had lost our parents at a young age, and that shared hardship allowed us to form a strong bond. However, your mother's life was rougher in many ways. When she was eight, she was taken in by an elderly aunt. At first, she thought she found a home with love until she realized that she was only there because the state sent a check to her aunt every month, and she was little more than a means of income for this woman." He continued. "Your mother suffered physical and mental abuse. She would spend hours, sometimes *days*, locked in what she referred to as the punishment room, nothing more than a broom closet. One day a teacher took her aside and asked why she had so many bruises on her hands and legs. She explained her aunt beat her with a switch because she didn't eat her dinner, which by the way, consisted of a butter sandwich on moldy bread and a half-rotten apple. Obviously, the teacher was horrified and immediately notified the authorities, and your mother became a ward of the state."

I sat in silence. While this didn't excuse my mother for how she treated me, it explained why she couldn't show me love. It was because she never knew what it was until she met my father. Thinking back, she'd spent years helping people get certified in fostering programs so they could take care of the troubled kids coming into their homes. She had always been invested in personally ensuring a safe and healthy living environment for the kids who had entered the system. It still astounded me that she could so easily look down her nose at Frankie and his family, everyone really, even though she'd come from nothing herself.

"Your mother wanted to pursue a career in law and become a law guardian for children, to help represent and protect kids, so they didn't end up as she did. She was very driven to prove to everyone that a child in the system could become something with hard work and dedication. We both worked two jobs to make ends meet, and we didn't rely on anyone for help. When I turned twenty-one, I received a letter from an attorney that I was to inherit the money my parents had left behind in a trust. I never knew this existed, and it was a blessing because it meant we could move out of our one-bedroom apartment and into a nicer area. Things seemed to be looking up for us. She was accepted into law school, and I was just hired on to work for a local assemblyman as his assistant."

My mind was reeling, but looking back, the words he said next were the ones I'd waited years to hear. They were the words that would finally help me solve the puzzle of her resentment toward me.

"One day, I came home early to surprise her with a romantic dinner and tell her I was going to run for City Council. There was a message on the answering machine from her doctor regarding blood work saying he needed to speak to her right away. Worried something was wrong, I played the message for her when she came home. I wanted her to talk to me, tell me what had happened, but she was very evasive and said it was nothing, probably just the anxiety medicine she was taking and nothing more. Several days later, she went to the doctor and afterward met me for lunch," he said, releasing a long sigh as he stared off into space, the memory taking a firm grip on him as he spoke. "She was stone-faced, emotionless as she sat across from me that day. I asked her what was wrong, and she finally admitted that she was pregnant. We were kids. I was scared, but I knew we'd created you with love and figured that had to mean something," he said, squeezing my hand. "Instead, she said she wasn't ready to be a mother. She couldn't give a child what it needed emotionally and physically, and it wasn't fair. She planned to terminate the pregnancy before it was too late." His eyes were filled with guilt, shame and what was worse—pain. "I was so shocked at her reaction that we fought for days, Lexi."

His voice trailed off, and for the first time since he began, I finally spoke.

"Daddy, it's okay. I needed to hear this," I said, squeezing his hand. "I think I finally understand a little better now, and although it hurts, it's nothing compared to what I'd felt before, never knowing anything at all."

"I wanted to marry her and raise a family, but she wanted no part of that. Finally, I managed to break down the walls she built around her heart, and we agreed to get married and raise you together. At six months pregnant, she began having complications and was unable to keep up with the demands of law school, so she had to drop out. In my job as an assistant, I was learning all about politics and how it worked. I knew I wanted a career helping the people, so I started to get more involved with committees and getting my name out there. This also put a wedge between us because I was never home, and her depression and anxiety became much worse."

"Daddy, it wasn't your fault," I said, giving him the most reassuring smile that I could manage. "You had a family to take care of."

"I know, Lexi, but she was my wife. I should have been more attentive to her needs instead of focusing so heavily on my career when I knew she needed me. That's where I failed as a husband," he admitted, his voice filled with shame. "You finally came, and the day you were born was the happiest of my life. Watching you take your first breath, holding you... nothing else mattered. The love I had from that moment on was something I cannot explain. You will understand when you hold your child for the first time," he promised, finally smiling. "Having a new baby and no family to help us, we had to rely on each other for everything. I continued to make a name for myself and build my career while your mother stayed home and took care of you. Postpartum depression started to engulf her. She did the best she could, but she was struggling. We fought all the time, and she would shut down. We were living like roommates who hardly spoke. She would get jealous if I paid too much attention to you, mad if I was too tired to take over when I came home. There was no winning. It had become an unhealthy home to raise a child in. After begging her for months, she sought help and started to come around, I thought there was hope. When you were a year old, I ran for the State Representative seat and won. She was thrust into the limelight of politics and loved it. She finally had a way to help people, something she always wanted to do. However, balancing being a mother and wife of a politician was too much for her, so once again, she began to struggle. One day, a local girl who had been a part of my campaign committee had fallen on hard times and came to me to see if she could get help from the state. She was looking for affordable housing and gainful employment. With your mother trying to juggle both a baby and helping me build my career, it often left her exhausted and overwhelmed. We discussed it and decided we were able to give this young woman a roof over her head and a job if she helped take care of you."

"Audrina?" I asked, choking back the tears.

"Yes, Lexi. Audrina was a godsend in many ways," he nodded, releasing another deep breath, steeling himself for the rest. "My biggest failure as her husband and your father was never seeing her pull away from us until it was too late. She'd taken on the role of a politician's wife to perfection and forgot she had a family. Over the years, we became more and more distant. However, in front of the cameras, we seemed to be the perfect family. The physical aspect of our marriage was gone and had been for some time," he admitted, raking his palm over his jaw. "One night after a few glasses of wine, she admitted she didn't love me anymore, but she'd never divorce me because she didn't want the shame and publicity. She reminded me of the dreams she gave up for us. She felt she was owed this for her sacrifices, but divorce was not an option for her. She said if I needed a companion, she would turn a blind eye," he said, rubbing his face in exhaustion before finally looking back at me once more. "Falling in love was easy, Lexi. Keeping that love strong was the hard part."

My head was spinning. I stood and made my way over to the window, doing what I could to gather my thoughts and emotions. This was a punch in the stomach, but I needed to close this chapter no matter how painful. He slowly rose from his chair and joined me in silence as we both stared out into the darkness.

"Lexi, I am sorry," he said quietly, turning toward me. "I know you blame your mother, but we've both failed you in so many ways."

Looking up at him, tears streaming down my face, I finally let out what I had been holding back for years.

"I have spent my entire life trying to be the perfect daughter, to make her proud and she gave me nothing in return. I would lie in bed at night and pray for her love, never knowing that God answered my prayers by giving me Audrina, who did love me and raised me to be the woman I am today. Not her," I said, swiping my tears. "I now know why she despised the Moretti's. They are what a real family should be, and she could not stand that. I am sorry you had to stay in a marriage without love for the sake of me. I've never doubted your love. I needed you more," I admitted. "I was helpless. I was a child, and she had demons that, until this moment, I had no idea just how many of them I had to pay for." The sob in my chest threatened to take over, but my determination to finish was stronger. "I pray that wherever she is, she finds peace, but she can't hurt me anymore. I'm done letting her tarnish the love I have for you."

Chapter Seven

Gia

As Shelby and I listened to Lexi's recap of the conversation she'd had with her father, we couldn't help but feel terrible for our friend. We'd both been lucky enough to come from loving families, so the thought of finding out your mother was jealous and resentful over sacrificing a career for her child wasn't something we could understand. However, when she was finished telling us everything, it was impossible not to notice the relief in her eyes with finally knowing none of it had been her fault.

Later that night, I had a date with Colin. I felt horrible asking Lexi to help me, especially after what she had just been through, but I was desperate. It had been a long time since I'd been with someone. I had a feeling we'd finally be having sex, and I wanted to make sure I had everything in place. After all, it wasn't every day I unveiled my pride and joy.

"Lexi, I am so fucked," I said as I walked into her room, securing the towel wrapped around me, and taking a seat on the edge of her bed in frustration. "I don't have a clue what to wear tonight. What happens if he actually *does* want to sleep with me, and I suck?" I released a low, dramatic sigh and rested my chin in my palm, admitting defeat. "Maybe I should just cancel and become a fucking nun."

"You? A nun? You wouldn't last a week. You know they don't let them swear, right?" Lexi balked. "Just relax. Stop trying to force the sex thing, just let it happen naturally. Once Shelby is done talking to her mom, we'll help you pick out something amazing to wear. We've got your back, Gia. Don't worry."

"Thanks, Lexi." I smiled at her. "I know the last thing you needed today is a neurotic friend wearing on your last nerve."

"Gia, it's okay to be a little scared. I was the same way with Frankie."

"Oh, my God," I shook my head, my eyes closing as I feigned nausea. "Lexi, please. A mental picture of my brother banging my best friend is the *last* thing I need right now."

"Stop being so dramatic, you weirdo." She laughed.

"What's so funny?" Shelby asked, stepping inside.

"Gia needs help getting ready for her date," Lexi explained, standing to move toward her closet. "We're going for 'hottie' not 'hooker.'"

After a half hour of trying on different outfits, I settled on a black jumpsuit halter with wide pant legs and a pair of Valentino's. I swept my hair off to the side in a mass of curls, and when I was finished, I felt beautiful and sexy. I just hoped Colin thought so, too. If not, I was going to give him a swift kick in the nuts with my spikes and leave him with the lasting memory of Gia Moretti.

"Colin's here," Lexi said with a wink as she stuck her head in.

I took a second to compose myself before I finally stepped out, the first peek of him taking my breath all over again. He was in a grey Armani suit that fit him perfectly. When he heard my heels clicking across the marble, his eyes rose to meet mine, and his lips turned into the most gorgeous smile, making his emerald eyes sparkle. I gave him a goofy wave, inwardly kicking myself for being such an awkward idiot before I carefully took each step with *Gia's getting laid* chanting in my head. When I finally reached the last step, he met me, extending his hand.

"Gia, you look stunning," he said, staring at me. "I am a man of many words, but tonight I find myself speechless."

"Thank you," I said, taking in his tousled hair and flawless face.

I'd always vowed to not date anyone better looking than me, but Colin was hot as hell and proof that sometimes rules were made to be broken.

I just hoped it didn't come back and bite me in the ass.

"Are you ready?" he asked, his voice husky as his eyes roamed me like his prey. "I've got a lot of plans for you tonight. I don't want to waste a second."

Jesus Christ. I think Maggie just burst into flames.

Colin thought of everything. The private table he'd reserved for us in the back of the restaurant made it feel like we were in our quiet little world. We talked about anything and everything. I loved that being with Colin was so easy. For once in my life, I felt like I'd found something that was real.

After our dinner and several glasses of wine, I was starting to feel just the perfect amount of tipsy—loose, but not too drunk for what I knew was coming next. I was ready.

"Shall we?" Colin started, pulling a nod from me. "I booked us a room at the Belmond. No pressure. We can just spend the night enjoying each other's company if that's what you'd prefer," he offered, standing and reaching for my hand. "Maybe just let me get a few cheap feels in. Nothing you wouldn't let me do on a normal day."

"Sounds perfect," I said, reaching to meet his lips before pulling away, walking a little too fast toward his car.

Fuck it, I thought. *Who cares if I look penis deprived? I'm getting laid.*

The hotel was breathtaking. The entrance featured an ornate fountain with bronze horses at its base, while the lobby was practically draped in Italian marble leading to the opened arm staircase in the center.

The elevator ride was quiet, Colin holding my hand and staring out straight ahead like a man on a mission. When the doors finally opened, my heart was pounding as we made our way to our suite. He ushered me inside, and the formal living room that waited just beyond the door made me stifle a gasp. I came to a slow stop, rose petals leading a path toward the bedroom that held a king size bed. My nerves began to take over once more before his arm wrapped around my waist, his fingertips calming me instantly.

"Gia, from the first time we spoke, you challenged the man inside me. No one else has ever done that," he admitted, his hot breath on my neck as I felt him brush against my ass, sending a jolt of need through me. "I'm thankful every day that you've come into my life."

His lips moved over my neck, making my knees weak as I leaned into him.

"I feel the same way for you," I confessed, trying not to lose my nerve as I slowly turned in his arms, resting my palms on his chest. "I'm not sure I ever knew what love was until we met." The word slipped out before I could stop it, and I felt my mouth go dry in panic. "I know I said love. Don't freak out," I managed with a nervous smile. "I've just always heard when you know you've finally gotten it right, the word finds new meaning every day."

"Gia, the word love doesn't scare me," he whispered, searching my features before his eyes fell back to mine. "It only scares me to think about how much I love *you*." Before I could respond, his lips were on mine. The way he cradled my neck as his tongue tasted me made my head spin. I gripped his shirt, kissing him back just as hard until, finally, we both pulled away, breathless. "Why don't you go get comfortable, and I'll pour us some wine?"

I nodded and moved toward the bathroom, locking the door and resting my back against it.

"Okay, Gia," I whispered to myself as I took a step in and found my reflection in the mirror, ready to give myself the pep talk of all pep talks. "Don't fuck this up. You have the world by the balls with this guy. You have primped, trimmed, and scrubbed every body part for this moment."

I gave myself a quick once-over, grateful to find I still looked pretty good. I reached into my overnight bag, horrified to find I forgot to pack my toiletry shit. My toothbrush, deodorant, makeup all missing. I was so worried about my underwear matching my bra that I forgot all my shit on the counter at Lexi's house.

I swear to God, someone up there doesn't want me to get laid.

I was dangerously close to tears when I found a pack of gum in the bottom of my bag and shoved four pieces into my mouth. There was no time for a full shower, so quickly, I grabbed a face cloth on the counter and decided to use that to freshen up as quickly as possible. By the time I finally sat down to pee, the wine and adrenaline were hitting me full force, making my head go in a million different directions all at once.

"Okay, it's go-time," I whispered to myself before spitting my gum into the tissue and cleaning myself up.

Instantly, I knew I'd made a mistake.

"Oh, fuck!" I whispered harshly, glancing down to find the sticky glob glued to Maggie. "Oh, my God!" I said in a low panic, as tried like hell to not hyperventilate. "Okay, Gia. Just stay calm. You just have to pull it off."

With a sharp tug, I yanked at the gum, getting most of it off despite the pain and muffled profanity that followed. A quick glance showed me there was still some *attached*. Once I realized it was only getting worse, I reached for my phone to call in reinforcements.

"Gia?" Lexi answered, her voice sounding worried. "Is everything okay?"

"No, Lex," I admitted, resting my head against the wall beside me. "I'm in trouble. I need your help."

As quickly and as quietly as I could, I explained my hell, their laughter nearly deafening as it poured out of my phone.

"I hate you both!" I hissed into the phone. "Stop fucking laughing and help me! My vagina is sticky as fuck, and it smells like peppermint!"

"Well, it gives new meaning to double your pleasure," Shelby said, laughing even harder.

"What am I going to do?" I demanded, almost in tears. "I can't have sex with gum stuck to my vagina! Why does this shit always happen to me?"

"Gia, just relax," Shelby said as if she'd been through the same thing a million times before. "Just have them bring up some peanut butter and use that or ice to get it off."

"Seriously, Annie Oakley? That's all you got right now? Call room service?" I balked. "And say what? Please bring a jar of peanut butter to four-fifteen? We've got a situation with a gummy vagina? Fuck no!"

"Gia?" Colin called from the other side of the door, making my eyes widen in terror. "Are you alright? Who are you talking to?"

"Shit! I have to go, he's at the door. Thanks for nothing, assholes," I hissed into the phone, shaking my heads at their laughter. "Yes, Colin. I'm fine," I lied. "Lexi called needing something. I'll be right there."

I bent to pull my panties up. Immediately, I knew it was worse.

Gathering what was left of my dignity, I opened the door and found him waiting for me, drinking wine on the velvet couch across from me as soft music played in the background. He was perfect, but with every step I took toward him, the tugging of the fabric on my skin was another reminder of the humiliating disaster in my pants. When I plopped onto the couch beside him in frustration, he held his wine glass up to avoid spilling it, looking at me like I was crazy.

"Are you okay?" he asked, his eyebrows scrunched together. "You couldn't have gotten into too much trouble in the bathroom. What happened with Lexi?"

"Oh, my God," I sighed, burying my face in my hands. "Okay, Colin. You said you loved me, right?" I started, glancing over to find him nodding in concern. "Well, I am about to test that right now."

"What's wrong?"

I held his eyes as he reached for my hand, the affectionate squeeze and his concern all it took for me to break.

"Gia," he said as the tears begin to fall over my cheeks. "Baby, you're freaking me out."

"I have…" I managed, my voice cracking before I finally crashed my head into his chest and fell apart completely. "I have gum stuck to my vagina!"

"*What*?" he asked, pulling me away from his chest. "You have *what* stuck *where*?"

"Gum," I blurted again, this time the sobs taking me full force. "On my vagina."

"Oh, my God!" he shouted, laughing hysterically as he pulled me onto his lap, shielding himself from my vengeance. "Baby, I'm all for kink, but this has got to be some new shit. I've never heard of using gum like that."

"No, dickhead!" I yelled, smacking him harder. "I left my toothbrush at Lexi's, and we ate all that garlic, so I chewed a bunch of gum and accidentally spit it out on the toilet paper I was using to wipe with. So now it's stuck!"

"Well, that *is* a sticky situation," he replied, still chuckling, blocking himself from my impending assault. "Calm down. I'll call room service. Maybe they've got some peanut butter or something."

"Great!" I rolled my eyes. "Another one with the fucking peanut butter."

"Baby, you are a wet dream and a nightmare all rolled into one," he smirked, pulling the phone to his ear, ordering the peanut butter before hanging up.

"Yeah? I'm leaning more toward a friggin' nightmare." I sighed, pulling his eyes back down to mine. "Listen, you should just dump my ass for a normal girl who doesn't have a double mint flavored vagina."

"Are you kidding me?" he asked, pressing his lips to my nose. "We're gonna be laughin' about this for years, babe."

A half-hour later, room service arrived with not only peanut butter, but chocolate covered strawberries with whipped cream, and champagne. I excused myself to the bathroom, ignoring Colin's overly eager offers of help as I locked the door behind me.

"Well," I said when I returned a few minutes later. "It's mostly gone, but I'm not letting you near me until I'm spotless."

"I understand." He smirked, feeding me a strawberry. "You know, just for the record, peanut butter and jelly is my favorite."

That time, I couldn't help but laugh with him.

What sucked big time was that I'd be heading back to Boston in two days, so God only knew when we would see each other again. We vowed to make this long-distance thing work and would do what we needed to do to keep the romance hot, but it didn't mean it was always easy.

After showering, I climbed into bed and rested my head on Colin's bare chest. I rubbed my nose along his jaw, inhaling his

Dolce and Gabbana cologne. I moved lower, swiping my tongue over his nipple.

"Gia, I don't think you..." he groaned as I placed my finger over his lips. Slowly, I straddled him, tossing my tank top to the side before exposing my breasts to him. He reached for them, and I caught his wrists in my hands, placing them over his head.

"Gia you're playing with fire."

Leaning forward, I slowly parted his lips searching for his tongue. Together, they did a lustful dance, Colin barely keeping his composure as he grabbed my hips and twisted into me.

"You're killing me," he panted.

"Shhh," I whispered.

"This is the only time you'll ever be in control," he warned with a husky laugh as he slapped my ass and rocked his hips into mine. "Enjoy it while you can, you little smartass."

I released a breathy laugh as I traced each ridge of his abs with my tongue, following the strip of hair that led the way with my fingertip. Tugging at the Armani band, I slowly pulled his underwear down, my mouth going dry as his throbbing cock sprung free. We'd fooled around before, I'd seen him stroke himself to orgasm for me over Skype as I pleasured myself more than once, but this was the first time I'd ever been able to touch the magnificent beast myself. I couldn't wait any longer.

I wrapped my lips around his tip, letting my tongue do all the work. I sucked and stroked him until his face morphed into pleasurable pain and I knew I hit the jackpot. His fingers brushed over my panties, slowly rubbing me until I was drenched with the need to have him inside me. We exploded together, both of us exhausted when we fell back against the mattress.

It was the first time in my life that I didn't feel dirty or cheap.

It was the first time I'd ever felt loved.

When we pulled up to Lexi's the next morning, their stupid grins made me want to smack them both in their smug faces.

"You two look very happy," Shelby said with a smile. "And I hope you brought your sweet tooth. Audrina's been baking cookies all morning just for you." She smirked. "They're peanut butter. Your favorite, Gia."

"Assholes," I grumbled as Colin, and I walked past them, ignoring their howls of laughter. "I hate both of you."

"Oh, come on, Gia. If that had happened to one of us, you would be all over our asses, and you know it," Lexi said, pulling me in for a side hug. "Besides, you have to admit. It's pretty funny. Even Frankie thought so."

"You told my *brother*?" I railed, pulling away from her. "Oh my God, is nothing sacred to you? Whatever happened to girl code, you bunch of asshats?"

"Well, that would explain the text I got from him this morning." Colin laughed, pulling his phone out of his pocket to show me the message.

> **Dude, I don't want to know how or what took place last night. Just make sure you take care of my baby sister or your minty ass is mine.**

We made our way into the kitchen to find Audrina finishing up the last of the cookies, and I popped one into my mouth, releasing a groan of appreciation.

"Well, Gia, I am glad you are enjoying the treats Audrina has made," Senator Cole said as he slowly approached the counter, cane in hand as Cynthia followed after him, her nose stuck into her iPad. My Spidey senses were tingling around those two. Something was going on. "If she keeps cooking like this, I'll have to loosen my belt another notch."

"Yes, sir. Thank you." I smiled at him, giving Lexi the stink eye. "I think they're wonderful."

"Senator Cole," Colin started, going in for the save. "My father would like to have the girls for one last dinner tonight before they head back to Boston. We'd love it if you'd join us."

"Son, that sounds wonderful. These old walls are starting to close in on me," the senator said, gently sitting down on the stool.

"Perfect." Colin smiled, reaching for another cookie. "Cynthia, you are more than welcome to join us as well."

"Thank you, Mr. McGrath. I appreciate the invitation, but I have plans for this evening," she said, nodding her head and offering a smile of appreciation for his hospitality. "Please just make sure to not overdo it, Jackson," she warned sweetly. "If you'll excuse me."

Lexi

"I'm not sure she knows the meaning of rest," Daddy said as Cynthia headed toward his office.

"Daddy, you should give her a raise," I said, my attention on the cookies in front of us. "She was incredible when you were in the hospital. Never mind how she worked with Angus setting up the wake and funeral. I would have been lost without..." I glanced up to find him watching her as she made her way across the hall, the lightbulb in my head going off almost instantly. Was she the woman he had found solace in all those years after my mother told him she no longer loved him? Even after I considerd it, I couldn't be mad at her. My mother treated her worse than the help. The only difference with her was that her abuse happened in public. Cynthia was like dirt on my mother's shoes for years, and now I thought I knew why.

"You okay, Lexi?" Shelby asked.

"Yes, I am fine. What time is dinner tonight, Colin?"

"Let's plan on seven. Pops is going to barbecue," he said, pulling Gia close and kissing her temple. "Nothing fancy. Just a relaxing dinner for his girls."

"Great, that gives us time to pack. We have an early morning flight," I said, walking over and putting my arm around my dad. "Are you sure I should be leaving so soon? You're just getting started to move around good on your own."

"Alexis, I am fine. I'm getting stronger every day. You have to get back to move into your apartment and get set for school," he said, standing and kissing my cheek. "No need to hang around here and babysit me. Besides, I have Carl, Audrina, and Cynthia to do that, sweetie. I hate to rush off, but I have a few calls to make and some corporate cages to rattle," he said, moving toward his office. "I may be injured, but that won't stop me from kicking some butt. Let's plan on being ready to head out for dinner at a quarter to seven."

"I'm gone, too, ladies. I've got to meet Jake to fill an order. Gia, come give me some sugar."

"Sugar this," Gia said, smacking her own behind. "You want a kiss, you come to me."

"Fine. I'll see you at seven sharp," he countered from the hallway.

"Colin McGrath, if you leave this house without kissing me goodbye, you're gonna regret it," Gia threatened from the kitchen.

Within seconds, Colin marched back into the kitchen, a lion on the verge of attacking its prey as he grabbed Gia and kissed her long and hard until she went completely limp in his arms.

"That ought to shut you up for a few hours," he said giving her a pleased reaction as he pulled away and smacked her hard on the ass. "Okay, off to work."

Gia

"That boy is so pussy whipped, it's ridiculous." I rolled my eyes as Lexi ended Frankie's fifth FaceTime call of the day.

Although I was sad to be leaving, unsure of when I'd see Colin again, I had to admit I was happy to be going home. I missed my mom and Nonna. What's more, Frankie said they'd finished moving the last of our things in today, but I was sure Lexi would have them rearrange everything three more times, so we had plenty to do once we touched ground in Boston.

When it was time for supper, we all waited in the foyer for Mr. Cole, the familiar ping of text coming from Shelby's phone.

She only looked at the screen for a moment before sliding her phone back into her pocket.

After all the shit with Lexi and her texts, I immediately went into defense mode.

"Everything okay, Shelbs?"

"Yeah, it was just a message from Colin's friend, Jake. He was just saying he looked forward to seeing me tonight."

"That's awesome," Lexi said, smiling like a loon. "From what I have seen he is such a nice guy!"

"Yeah, he seems to be, but how did he get my number? I didn't give it to him." Her eyes narrowed when we looked away awkwardly. "You guys gave it to him? He's married! Why would you do that?"

"Well, first of all, we don't *know* that he's married," I said defensively. "Second of all, you're not marrying the guy, for Christ's sake. Relax and just have some fun."

"Whatever," she said, moving toward Mr. Cole as he emerged in order to helped the senator with his coat. "But if I find out differently, I'm blocking his ass."

Shelby

As I helped Senator Jackson up the stairway that led us to Angus' door, the sound of a little girl's laughter came pouring out, growing louder as Colin opened the door to greet us.

"Jackson, you old son of a bitch," Angus said as he joined us, giving Lexi's father a gentle pat on the back. "We're so glad you could make it."

"I wouldn't miss one of your barbecues for the world, Angus. Besides, I am so sick of being stuck in the house, I would welcome a visit from the devil himself."

Their pleasant exchange was interrupted by the same angelic, blonde haired little girl who'd turned up at my desk earlier. Her full run came to an abrupt stop when she reached the corner and saw more guests had arrived, shyly hiding behind Jake's leg when he came to a stop beside her.

"Jake, you know the Senator and his daughter Lexi," Angus started, gesturing toward them. "These pretty ladies next to her are—"

"Yes, sir. I had the pleasure of meeting Shelby and Gia previously. It's great to see you all again." Stepping forward, Jake extended his hand to Jackson. "Senator, Lexi, please accept my deepest sympathy for your recent loss."

"Thank you, son, we appreciate your kind words. It's nice to see you again," Jackson replied, glancing down at Jake's daughter with a smile. "And who is this pretty little lady?"

"My name is Campbelle Montgomery, sir," she said, glancing up at Jake. "That's my daddy."

"Well, it's a pleasure to meet you, Campbelle. Are you here for dinner too?" Jackson asked, shaking her small hand.

"Yes, sir," she nodded, brave enough to take a step closer. "Do you want to play tag with us?"

"Campbelle, Mr. Cole isn't up to playing tag. Maybe next time." Jake smirked. "Where are your manners? You haven't said hello to Miss Shelby, Miss Gia, or Miss Lexi yet."

"Hello," she said, offering each of us her hand and a shy smile before turning back to her father. "Daddy, can I play until supper?"

"Yes, but mind your manners and don't get into anything," he said, watching her as she skipped back down the hall before returning his attention to us. "Sorry, she's a little wound up. Colin gave her candy."

"Well, you know I'm a sucker for a pretty lady," Colin said, giving Gia a kiss. "I'm not gonna deny that kid anything."

"Shelby, we meet again," Jake said, laughing nervously. "I swear I'm not a stalker."

"It's nice to see you again," I smiled, my stomach rolling with nerves as I faced him. "I'm looking forward to meeting your wife. She'll be joining us, won't she?"

"I'm afraid not," he said, glancing away slightly before clearing his throat and facing me again. "My wife passed two years ago. It's just Campbelle and me now."

Great. You've just insulted a widower. Smooth, Shelby.

Gia's elbow hit my ribs, pulling my narrowed gaze to hers and stopping her in her tracks.

"What?" she mouthed, making me roll my eyes before glancing back at Jake. "I had no idea, Jake," I admitted softly. "I am sorry for your loss."

"Thank you." He nodded, and the awkward silence that followed made me feel terrible.

Lexi sensed it and thankfully, came to my rescue.

"Angus, what did you make us tonight? I am starved."

"Pork shoulder, chicken, and peach cobbler for dessert, so I hope you brought an appetite," he said, making our mouths water as he led us inside. "Come on back to the patio and get yourselves a drink. We're gonna send you pretty girls home with full bellies."

124

Dinner was terrific. We laughed, and conversation flowed smoothly, Campbelle entertaining us throughout the night. I caught myself more than once looking over at Jake, and he would look my way and smile, causing me to blush like a dork. After having a couple of glasses of wine, I felt a little more relaxed, and I decided to flirt. We were leaving for Boston the next morning, so I figured no harm, no foul, right?

Once dinner was cleaned up, and Campbelle was sitting happily in Angus' office with dessert and cartoon, we all made our way outside by the fire pit with our drinks. Gia settled on Colin's lap, while Lexi chatted with Angus and her father about Frankie and the business. I considered talking to Jake but quickly lost my nerve, opting instead to walk to the edge of the patio and enjoy the sunset.

"You okay?" Jake asked, startling me just slightly as he joined me.

"Yes, I'm fine." I nodded, trying to deflect. "I just felt like moving around some."

"I understand you're heading back to Boston tomorrow," he said, kicking the rock beside his shoe into the yard. "I am sure your boyfriend will be happy to see you."

"Boyfriend." I chuckled to myself, glancing over at him. "The only one missing me in Boston right now is a horse named Gracie, and I'm pretty sure she's just using me for my carrots."

Jake's smile widened at my words before he angled himself a little closer.

"Do you believe in fate, Shelby?"

"I used to," I said, my voice quieter as I blinked back the sting of tears, praying he hadn't noticed. One look at him told me otherwise.

"You know, Shelby," he sighed, smiling down at me. "As cruel as fate can sometimes be, she can also be pretty good about giving away second chances. You just have to recognize them when they come." His words had my mind reeling, struggling for a response until he broke the silence once more. "We should get to know each other better. I'd like to be your friend."

"Sure." I smirked. "One can never have too many of those."

"Agreed." He nodded, offering me his hand and smiling as I shook it. "Friends it is."

We talked for hours until, sadly, it was time for the evening to come to an end. We gathered our things and said our goodbyes to Angus and Colin, my heart breaking for Gia. She tried to be the tough girl, but her tears gave her away.

"I hate this," Gia said, burying her head in his chest.

"I know, baby. I do, too, but I promise I will be up to see you soon," Colin said, wrapping his arms around her tight. "Business with your brother is booming so we'll both be back and forth," he said, lifting her chin and placing a kiss on her lips. "Don't cry, Gia. You're breaking my fucking heart."

Deciding to give them some privacy, Lexi and I helped Jackson get settled in the car.

"I wish I could do this on my own," Jackson admitted to Lexi under his breath as she helped him with his door.

"Daddy, you are doing great," Lexi said, kissing his cheek. "Your therapist is going to be here three days a week, and you will be back to your old self in no time."

"I would milk all this attention if I were you, old man," Angus said as he approached the car, bending down, shaking his hand, and giving him a wink.

"I know you would." Jackson laughed. "I will stop by next week and kick your ass in backgammon."

"Well, I need to get Campbelle home to bed," Jake said, joining us. "Thanks again, Angus, for the invite. It's nice to get out and make a new friend," he said, glancing at me and smirking as I blushed. "Being a single dad can get lonely sometimes."

"Been there, done that," Angus admitted. "Don't be a stranger. You're welcome anytime."

"Thanks," he said, looking at Lexi. "Nice to see you again."

"Thank you, Jake," she said, leaning over to give him a friendly hug. "It was wonderful seeing you, as well."

"Shelby," he said, taking my hand and kissing it gently as he held my eyes. "Keep in touch."

"O-okay," I stammered, the sweet gesture enough to leave me dumbfounded as my mouth went dry.

As he drove away, I caught him smiling at me through the rearview, setting the butterflies in my stomach off full-force.

The sound of Gia's laughter as she smacked Colin playfully on their way toward the car pulled my attention back, happy to see her feeling better.

"Okay, ladies. I'm ready," she announced, smiling at Colin.

"We'll miss you, girls," he said, coming to a slow stop beside us. "I'll be seeing you soon, though. You know I've got to keep that pain in the ass business partner of mine on his toes." He chuckled, leaning down to give Gia a final kiss goodbye, pinning her to the side of the car, making her pull away love-drunk a moment later.

"Alright, son. Enough mauling or she won't get on the plane," Angus teased, making us smile as we waved and said our goodbyes.

Tomorrow, we'd be back in Boston.

Chapter Eight

Lexi

While it was hard to leave my father the next morning, I knew he was in good hands with Cynthia, Audrina, and Carl. By the time we touched down in Boston, I was so excited to see Frankie that I texted him the second we hit the ground. All it took to have me out of my seat was a text back from him admitting he was waiting in baggage claim.

As I pulled my bag from the overhead, I glanced over at Shelby and Gia, watching their fingers fly wildly over the screen as they both wore goofy grins to match mine.

"Ladies, you ready to move into our brownstone?" I asked, gathering my stuff as we waited to step off the plane.

"Bet your ass," Gia exclaimed, moving to grab her things. "Thank god the boys moved all our stuff in while we were away. I know you're going to rearrange everything," —she smirked at me— "but at least we can sleep there tonight after we stop to see my mom and Nonna."

"Sounds good to me," Shelby said, not looking up from her phone. "I don't have to be at the stables until tomorrow. I'd love to see how the place looks and get settled."

"Who are you texting, Shelby?" Gia asked with a knowing smirk as she reached for her phone.

"Jake, nosy ass, I just wanted him to know we landed," she said, pulling the phone out of her reach. "Besides, if you think I didn't see the disgusting shit you were sending to Colin, you're wrong." She shuddered.

"Just wanted to remind him of what he's missing." She winked as doors to the plane opened.

Finally, I was going to see Frankie.

I practically ran the whole way to baggage claim.

Frankie

As she came down the escalator, I watched her search the crowd for me, taking a moment to just appreciate her innocent beauty. She had been through so much but always managed to see the good in everything. She had taught me to trust, love, and to finally be happy. When our eyes met, she waved, breaking into a smile and running into my arms.

I was finally whole again.

She melted into my arms as I kissed her fiercely, falling under her spell until...

"Jesus Christ, you two. Get a room!" Gia groaned, slapping my arm as she moved past me. "I actually saw your tongues touch that time."

"Missed you, too, sis," I said, mussing her hair and forcing her into a hug, reaching for Shelby and pulling her in, too, before releasing them and reaching for Lexi's bags. "Okay, girls. Let's get going. Ma and Nonna are waiting. I'm sure you're all hungry and ready to get to the apartment," I continued, winking at Lexi as I smacked her ass. "I know I am." Her lips moved into a wicked smile that immediately sent me into overdrive, pulling a low grumble from my chest. "Don't look at me like that. I'll drag your little ass into a closet."

"Promises, promises," she teased.

"Yeah? I can promise you'll be screaming my name tonight."

Gia

Ma and Nonna grilled me about Angus and Colin over dinner. I filled them in on what I could, but some of that shit they didn't need to know, especially the gum incident. I teased my mother about all her questions, asking if she had a girl crush on Angus.

"Gia, I do not have a crush on Angus McGrath," she insisted, fixing her shirt in a huff. *Did I imagine a blush?* "I found his company pleasurable, and seeing as you're dating his son, we have something in common."

"Theresa cut the shit." Nonna snorted as she rose with her plate. "You and I both know you had your face buried in that phone all week. Don't tell me you were texting Gia or Frankie because you giggled like a little school girl," she said, moving toward the sink. "Now, if you'll excuse me, I'm tired. Nurse Bella made me bend like a pretzel today and do shit my old body hasn't done in a long time. I'm going to sit my ass down and watch the news. I'm glad you girls are home," she said, winking at me as she kissed my hair. "Aside from this one giggling, it was too quiet around here."

As I watched her shuffle to her room, I couldn't help but smile to myself. Sure, she wasn't back to her old self, but she was getting closer every day, and her spirits were good. That was all that mattered.

"Ma, please tell me you are not flirting with Angus McGrath," Frankie groaned dramatically. "I can't have my entire family fooling around with my business partners."

"Frankie, I'm fifty-three. I don't flirt," she retorted, her expression annoyed as we began clearing the table. "And even if I were, he's doing business with Castagna, not you. Relax."

"Okay," he said, putting his hands up in retreat. "All I'm saying is I don't want you getting hurt and have it affect my business."

"*Your* business?" she asked her eyebrow quirking.

"You know what I mean." Frankie shrugged, reaching for Lexi's hand and leading her out.

"Frankie, what you are doing?" she asked, yelping as he pulled her out.

"Getting the fuck out of there before I blow my story," he admitted, smirking down at her. "Hey, speaking of blow…" He chuckled, throwing her over his shoulder and moving toward the stairs.

When they finally returned, Lexi was red-faced as she fell into the couch beside him, making me shake my head.

"Well, it's about friggin' time you two came down. I thought I was going to call for the Jaws of Life to pry two you apart," I teased.

"You're an asshole." Frankie shook his head, making us laugh.

"Don't get too comfortable, dick face. We want to go to the apartment. Get your shit together and drive us over there, please. I am sure the dynamic duo put stuff in the wrong places. I have already texted them to meet us there so we can arrange the shit properly."

"Calm down, bossy. Why do you think we're here?" he asked as he cuffed me in the back of the head and moved toward the door. "Stop your bitching and let's go."

Shelby

Listening to Gia and Frankie banter back and forth in the car was like watching a tennis match. They one-upped each other with sarcasm, one-liners flying everywhere. I considered recording it some days just so they could hear themselves, but I loved that no matter how bad they got, it was obvious that their love ran deep.

When we pulled up to the front of the building, we saw Mikey and Joey talking to three girls. Their backs were to us so I couldn't see their faces, but when we all jumped out and closed our doors, they finally turned around, making me stop in my tracks. It was Samantha, Stacy, and Beth from the barn. *What the hell are they doing here?*

"Hey, girls. How are you?" Joey said coming over and giving us all a hug, Mikey right behind him.

"We missed you, ladies. We hope you like what we did while you were away," Mikey said, looking back at the apartment.

Samantha stepped forward and stood next to Mikey.

"Shelly? What are you doing here? Wait, are you part of the cleaning service my parents hired?" she asked, wrinkling her nose at me.

"It's Shelby, you nitwit, and no," Gia snapped. "We live here. Who the hell are you?"

"We live here," she said, squaring her shoulders as Gia looked her up and down, clearly unimpressed. "We were just talking to our landlords, Michael and Joseph."

Gia snorted and rolled her eyes. "Wow," she said, feigning interest. "I had no idea my brother had hired these two to rent his house to douchebags."

"Samantha, Stacy, Beth," I interjected, trying to lighten the suddenly tense mood. "Looks like we're neighbors."

"Looks like it," Samantha sneered.

"So, this is Gia and Lexi. They're my roommates." I smiled, nervous as a growl left Gia's chest.

"Nice to meet you," Lexi said, stepping in front of us and extending her hand, flashing her pageant smile. "I am Alexis Cole."

"Yes, we know who you are," Stacy admitted. "We've seen you on campus. You're the senator's daughter, right?"

"Yep, that's right," Frankie answered for her, stepping between all of us. "And I'm the *other landlord* I'm sure you've heard so much about." He rolled his eyes toward Mikey and Joey before returning his attention toward the girls. "You've read and signed the lease?"

"Yes, Mr. Moretti. We are all set. I was just shocked to see Shelly... I mean *Shelby* here. Normally, I only see her at the stables where I ride." Samantha sighed, looking at me like I didn't belong on her side of the street.

"Well, now you'll see her next door," Frankie quipped, shutting her down quickly.

"Yes, we will. Thank you," she replied, glancing at Mikey. "If you need to reach me, you have my number. Come on, girls. Let's go unpack."

We watched her and her minions make their way inside, and simultaneously, our heads turned toward Mikey and Joey.

"Mikey, what the fuck?" Gia started, smacking him. "Please tell me you are not dipping your dick in that ice princess."

"She's not that bad, Gia." He rolled his eyes. "Besides, did you ever think maybe the problem is that you bring out the worst in people?"

He turned around and left, jogging toward the apartment and leaving Gia speechless—no easy feat.

"Come on," I started gently. "I have to work, and she boards her horse with us. I don't want any issues."

"Fine," she sighed, turning to face me. "Shelby, if you can promise me one thing, I swear I'll keep my mouth shut."

"Of course." I shrugged. "Anything."

"Don't take any shit from that girl. Just because she was born with a silver spoon up her ass, she has no right to treat you with disrespect. If you can promise me that, I'll keep my word."

"I agree," Lexi chimed in, wrapping her arm around me. "Don't let anyone talk down to you."

"I promise." I smiled, grateful for both their support and protectiveness. "I might just be nicer about it than Gia."

"Fair enough," she chuckled, grabbing our hands and pulling us along beside her. "Alright, ladies. Let's check out the new digs."

Three months later...

Gia

Things couldn't have been going better for us in the new apartment. Not only was it a relief to taste the freedom that came with no RA's or rules, but the three of us were also on-track to hit the Dean's list. Business at Castagna was booming, so much, in fact, that Frankie hired Lexi to help out. Even though they'd spent most days in his office *taking care of business*, it was still great to have the extra help.

Although it had been a total shock at first when Colin finally confirmed my suspicions that my brother, Mikey, and Joey were all the new owners of Castagna. It helped things click into place. I was pissed Frankie didn't tell me on his own, but at the same time, I appreciated Colin's respect for both his business with Frankie and his relationship with me, eager to keep them separate. At the end of the day, I was just happy and grateful that he'd stepped up and had done what was necessary to provide and take care of all of us. It had been a risk, for Frankie more than anyone, but thank God it had paid off in the end.

My mother still had no idea, and I knew it wasn't my place to tell her. After all that went down with my father, she still had a slightly bitter taste in her mouth, and I honestly couldn't blame her. I wasn't sure how she'd handle learning Frankie had lied to her all along, but I did know that when he was ready to come clean, I'd stand beside him knowing he did what he thought was best for all of us.

After all, that was what families were for.

With the holidays quickly approaching, Ma was always a little crazy, but adding Colin and Angus only amped her battiness. I'd asked her if something was going on with Angus, but she was still tightlipped, replying instead with some run-of-the-mill babble in a failed attempt to run me off. "It has nothing to do with impressing Angus, Gia," she insisted. "It's called being a good hostess."

I called bullshit. My money was on that fact that she had a crush on him. Who wouldn't? He was very handsome.

I knew we'd miss Shelby over Thanksgiving, but I was glad to see she was finally moving on after Drew. She swore up and down that taking Jake and Campbelle to Montana to meet her family was little more than a friendly visit, but we both knew better. In fact, it seemed most of the women in my life had an abundance of bullshit flying around when it came to men, but as long as she was happy, that was all that mattered to me.

One of the few that I could count on to be straight with me about her love life, much to my dismay, was Lexi. The best part about the change in her was the peace she'd found since her mother passed away. Craig had let her be and had accepted that things between them were over, and since we'd returned home, she hadn't received a single threatening text.

It seemed all was finally right in our tiny little corner of the world.

It was funny how the universe worked.

Just as things were finally falling into place, it decided it was time to shit on all of us at once.

Lexi

After the first few months of learning the ropes at Frankie's company, I was excited when he asked if I was ready to take on more. What didn't excite me was the prospect of working with Paige, learning how to rent and sell the units they were fixing up. However, I knew I had to give it a try if I would ever be able to enjoy my newfound passion for taking something old and tattered and breathing new life into it.

Paige and I had been working together for about a month, everything amicable, when she finally broke the ice and mentioned she'd been seeing someone. Of course, I'd been supportive, eager as ever to keep things civil with Frankie's ex, but her overzealous behavior had me wondering just how genuine she was being.

"This project is going to be a winner," she said, tapping the folder to an old warehouse Frankie and the McGrath's had recently purchased for loft conversions. "I can feel it in my bones. The real estate comp in the area is outrageous. It's a great location with an attached parking garage," she continued. "It also sits right across from the waterfront and is close to the Seaport district. If they succeed in selling out all the units, it will skyrocket their business to a whole new level."

"I agree. I'm looking forward to helping design the units with them, but first, we have to get past all the permits with the city. If everything's good to go, we should be able to start breaking down walls in less than a month."

"You're absolutely right," she said, glancing down at her phone as it blared. "Excuse me. I have to take this."

"No problem." I smiled, pulling my own phone out to check my texts, grinning when I saw messages from both Frankie and Gia.

Hey, babe. I am just checking in with you. How it's going with Paige?

Great, it seems we finally got the monkey out of the way (you) and are working towards the common goal of making everyone rich.

I am already rich. I have you.

True, but we cannot live on sex alone. I need food.

Oh, don't worry. I have a foot long just waiting for you back here.

Good Lord, you need help. Goodbye.

See you soon, baby.

I exited out of the screen and moved onto the next, smiling at Gia's text.

Hey, are you coming back to the office? Ma wants us for dinner tonight. She is making

lazy man subs. I'm not sure you've ever had them, but they're fucking awesome. She puts thick sliced layers of Italian bread in a baking dish with sliced meatballs on top and loads them with cheese before she bakes them. Then, you cut the bitch out in squares and pour sauce over them. So good!

Sounds very fattening. I am so in! I will be back in an hour. I am with Paige going over the waterfront project.

Sounds like torture

It's actually going pretty well right now. Apparently, there's a new boyfriend.

Thank God! She was becoming pathetic there for a while. See you in a bit. I will text Shelby to meet us at the house when she is out of class.

"Sorry about the interruption. It was my boyfriend calling about our plans for tonight," she admitted, glancing at me with a nervous laugh. "Is Frankie checking up on us?"

"No, it was Gia," I said, not feeling comfortable giving her any more than that as I put my phone back in my purse.

"Please tell her I said hi." Paige smiled, pulling out the rental information and marketing tools she was going to use to sell the waterfront. "Okay. Let's get back to work on these condos."

Gia

The smell of meatballs and sauce knocked me right on my hungry ass as I walked inside. Frankie and Lexi were right behind me making groaning noises. I thought it was because they were hungry, however, when I turned around, they slipped into the front room, making me roll my eyes.

"Are you kidding me right now?" I yelled from the hall. "It's bad enough you've bent her over that desk so many times that maintenance had to come in a bolt the thing to the floor."

Stepping out of the room with a smirk and holding Lexi's hand, Frankie pushed past me.

"You're just jealous because I have the real thing and you only have Skype," he said, laughing.

"Frankie, that's not nice," Lexi said, slapping him.

"Whatever, douchebag," I said, placing my bag on the counter and immediately following my nose toward the bread that was already cut and ready to be dipped in the sauce.

"Oh, my God." I laughed, catching the sauce as it dripped down my chin. "If I don't eat sauce once a week, I swear to God I get weak."

"Gia, get your paws out of my sauce, you little shit," Ma threatened, coming around the corner.

"Hey, Ma." I smiled, stuffing the last piece in my mouth. "How was work today?"

"Good, I just can't keep up with the clients," she admitted, settling onto her stool with her coffee. "I have to hire two more hairdressers and maybe start looking for a bigger place."

"That's great, Ma." Frankie beamed, kissing her cheek.

"It is, but I am getting to a point where I don't know if I want to do that," she said, stretching her arms over her head. "I am not a spring chicken anymore. I want to slow down a little."

"Why don't you hire someone to help you manage the shop?" Lexi suggested, grabbing plates from the cabinet. "You'd still make your profit by renting out stations and with your commission, but it would keep you from taking on extra work."

"I like that idea, Lexi. I will have to think about it. It could work if I hired the right person," she said kissing her cheek.

"Hello!" Shelby yelled from the hallway, dropping her bag and pulling each of us into a hug. "Oh, my God! It smells like heaven in here." Just then, Nonna came out of her room with her cane, swearing, mumbling about how she hated when the commentators shit all over the Patriots, and Belichick had to hold a press conference to answer stupid questions.

"Hey, sweet cheeks," I said, patting Nonna's ass as she came into the kitchen.

"You wish you had an ass like mine," she said tapping her cane against my leg.

"Nonna, the last thing I need is a mental image in my head of your ass," Frankie said, hugging her.

"I may be old and on my last leg, but you forget that the front room is next to mine. I heard some things a while ago coming from your mouth, and I think I just might have to pull out the rosary for the two of you." Nonna winked as she took her seat. "Now, enough of this chit-chat," she raised her eyebrow. "I'm hungry."

After dinner, Frankie and Lexi went upstairs while Nonna entertained us with stories about Nurse Bella, swearing she was on the verge of unemployment.

"Not only is she fresh to me, but I swear to God she is obsessed with my bowels," she exclaimed, slapping the table dramatically. "Theresa, you should find me a new nurse."

"It took me a month to find this one." Ma shook her head. "Just because she doesn't take your shit doesn't mean she's out. Kathie is a perfect fit."

"Whatever, you're all against me. I am going to watch TV," she threw her hands up, rising from the chair and blowing us a kiss before patting her hand on her ass.

"You've been awfully quiet, Shelby," Ma said, following her toward the sink. "How're things going with Jake? Are you excited to take him back to the ranch?"

"Yes, it will be fun. I am going to do some sightseeing and show Campbelle how to ride . He will also get to meet Christian and hang with him and Mike," she said nonchalantly.

"Shelby," I scoffed. "You've been texting that boy since you got back, and he's going to meet your family. It's a big deal."

"We're just friends." She rolled her eyes.

"Do you like him, Shelby?" Ma asked, making her reluctantly nod.

"I do," she admitted, biting her lip. "I'm just not... I'm not ready for more yet."

Since we'd returned, she'd finally come clean to us all about what had happened between her and her high school sweetheart, Drew. We knew it would be hard, but some days, I guess I took for granted that her talking about it had meant she'd moved on. Today must have been one of those days.

"I'm sorry, Shelby," I said, moving closer to pull her into a hug as I saw her eyes begin to tear up. "I didn't mean to make you cry. I just want you to be happy."

"I know." She nodded. "I'll be okay. I just need a little more time."

"Drew must've been pretty special to leave such a permanent mark on your heart," Ma whispered as she rubbed her shoulders. "When I lost my husband, I thought for sure I'd never love again. It was as if a piece of my soul went right along with him, but mourning a memory? That's no way to keep someone alive. If Drew loved you like I suspect he did, he'd want you to live your life. To be happy." She sighed, looking over her features. "And sometimes, that comes along when we least expect it."

"Thank you." She smiled, wiping her cheeks as her phone pinged, the image on the screen making her grin widen even further. "Look, its Campbelle." She beamed. "She asked Jake to send me this picture of her being a cowgirl."

"She's a doll." Ma laughed.

"She is. She'll be roping in no time," Shelby agreed. "Half the battle is not being afraid. She's far from that."

At that moment, I only wished I could say the same for Shelby.

Chapter Nine

Lexi

Frankie was leaning against his truck, reading his email and waiting for me when I got out of class, utterly oblivious to what was happening around him. Between his dark wavy hair, the scruffy beard he said he was growing to keep him warm in the winter, and his broad shoulders stretching the flannel shirt he wore, I wasn't the only one enjoying the mouthwatering view. Strolling towards him, I silently thanked God for bringing him to me.

"Hey, handsome."

"Hey, you." He smiled, pushing off the truck and bending down, kissing me like he knew that was exactly what I needed.

Pulling away, he grabbed my hand and squeezed it. We were going to see Officer Walsh today regarding another anonymous tip, and I, for one, could think of a hundred things I'd rather be doing. If I were the daughter of anyone else, this case could have been closed months ago, but with the backlash coming from the press should they get wind, I was at the mercy of discretion.

"You ready for this?" Frankie asked, looking at me with concern.

"I guess. It's not like they know who did it," I said in frustration. "Going down to the police station every time they think it's a solid lead never goes anywhere, and it's getting old, fast. How much longer do I have to do this?"

"Baby, we will do it a million times if we have to until this fucker gets locked up," Frankie promised, looking up at me.

"Fine, let's go and get it over with," I sighed, hopping into his truck.

"Miss Cole, Mr. Moretti," Officer Walsh greeted us once we arrived. "Thank you for coming down to talk with me."

Entering his office, it brought back memories of my attack. My heart began to race, and my mouth went dry from the anxiety. Immediately, I reached for Frankie's hand looking for comfort.

He took it, giving me the reassurance that I needed.

Officer Walsh folded himself in his chair, leaning forward clasping his hands together.

"I am just going to get right to point. Last week, I received another anonymous email with a videotape showing a car we believe the attacker was driving during the night of your attack. The college has security devices in place at the gate which register all vehicles that come on campus, and this was one that was not registered with the school, which is why it was flagged," he explained, leaning back in his chair.

"Is this anonymous person someone who works at the college?" Frankie said looking confused.

"We are not sure," Walsh explained. "The IP address the email came from matches the same one from which we received the blurry video clip showing the attack. We traced it back to a laundry service in China Town. Whoever this person is, they know how to keep their anonymity."

"Do you think this will help solve who did it?" I asked, wringing my hands nervously.

"We hope so, Miss Cole. We want nothing more than to find this person and prosecute," he said, closing the file. "We'll be sure to keep you and the senator very closely informed on any other developments."

"Thank you, Officer Walsh. I appreciate all the hard work and effort your team has put into this. I know my father can be relentless in getting what he wants, but I do hope you understand that he is just protecting his only daughter as you would your own if in the same situation." I smiled before shaking his hand and turning to Frankie. "Come on, babe. Let's go so he can work."

"Fine." He shook his head, clearly just as frustrated as me. We started to leave, but he whipped around and faced Officer Walsh once more. "You call us as soon as you hear something, you got it? I don't want to put her in any more danger because people are dragging their feet."

"Mr. Moretti, is it?" Walsh started, setting the file on top of the already intimidating stack on his desk. "As I said before, we will contact Ms. Cole and her father as soon as we determine if this vehicle and its owner have anything to do with the attack."

"Thank you again," I managed, tugging Frankie toward the door with me before he did anything stupid. "I look forward to hearing from you."

"Asshole," Frankie muttered as we pulled the door shut behind us.

I couldn't have agreed more, but I also didn't want to spend the afternoon trying to figure out how to bail my boyfriend out of jail. We made our way outside to his truck, and Frankie opened my door. Once I was inside, he stepped around front, his hand slamming on the hood loud enough to make me jump. He took a minute to pace outside before he finally blew out a breath and slipped behind the wheel, glancing over at me.

"If that prick thinks it's okay to let the fucker who did this shit to you just roam around Boston, he's sadly mistaken, Lexi." He shook his head, quietly fuming. "It's his job to make sure you're safe. If he refuses to do it, then I will."

"Frankie, I'll be fine," I whispered, my eyes pleading as I reached for his hand. "Nothing has happened to me since that night. We just have to let them do their job."

"Those text messages are no joke, Lexi," he disagreed. "I know they've stopped, but that doesn't mean shit."

"I know, Frankie, but they're close to catching them, and we'll be able to put it all behind us soon enough. No more looking over our shoulder or worrying every time my phone goes off," I reasoned, releasing a tired breath. "It's almost over. We just have to be patient a little while longer, okay?"

"Fine," he sighed, squeezing my hand before reaching to crank the ignition and glancing back over at me. "But if something happens to you, I'm gonna lose my shit."

Gia

I was almost to my economics class when I felt my phone buzz in my pocket. I considered looking at it, but if I was late for Professor Wilson's class again, I knew she'd make my life a living hell. She hated me, the scathing look that she gave me as I stepped inside making it all the more obvious, so whoever needed me would have to wait. My phone buzzed two more times while I was in class, and I'd assumed it was just one of the girls, but when I packed up my things and started to head out, I glanced down and stopped dead in my tracks.

Meet me at one o'clock alone at the bench where your friend was attacked. I have some information. If you aren't alone, you get nothing.

My hands were shaking as I looked at the clock. That was only fifteen minutes.

Who is this?

I got no reply, and my mind went into overdrive. I wasn't sure what to do. Should I risk going alone? Should I tell Frankie and risk the mystery informant not showing up? A million question flew through my mind, but before I could decide, I was already at the bench. No one was there, just the usual handful of students coming and going, which made me feel a little better. *Too many witnesses to do much harm,* I thought to myself as I pulled out my phone.

I am here alone.

I'd barely put my phone down before I felt a hand on my shoulder, making me jump as I turned, my mouth falling open in shock.

"No fucking way," I shook my head.

"Don't make a scene," she warned. "I know you don't like me, and I don't care, but I have a job to do here, and this shit with your friend is getting in the way."

"Your job?"

"Yes, Moretti. You didn't actually think I was a student here, did you?" she scoffed, shaking her head. "Anyway, I've been the one giving the police their tips, but they're spending so much time trying to track me down, they're not going after the person responsible, and I've been wasting time covering my tracks. I figured since you have such a big mouth, you'd help me move this shit along so that I can get back to what I'm actually supposed to be doing."

"Well, first of all, yes, I thought you were a student, Colleen. You were my roommate, for Christ's sake." I made a face. "Second, what the hell are you talking about, your job?"

"I was hired to help watch for security breaches within the school's firewall," she started. "Students like you who don't give a shit and just click on any link you see make it all vulnerable to hackers, and I have to sweep in behind you so that your information is protected. There are people on campus constantly trying to hack into the system to change shit. A few have even been successful enough to demand payment to avoid leaking private information and have walked away with full pockets and no charges filed against them. If you could see some of the shit I pull off these videos, you'd be sick." She shook her head, finally meeting my eyes.

"You saw who attacked Lexi, didn't you?" I asked, chills running over me.

"Yes," she nodded, reaching for her phone. "I went to the police immediately, but the angle was off so the image I captured was blurry and it was hard to identify them. After scouring through the video from the main gate, though, I found something that would help," she said, handing me her phone. "The car used during the attack is registered to Paige Matthews, your brother's ex."

"Oh, my God," I whispered, taking in the photo and recognizing it immediately as Paige's car.

"I sent this to the police. I know your friend met with them today, but they're dragging their feet. I don't have anything on her from the actual attack, but my gut tells me it was her. Why else would she have been on campus?"

"I have to call my brother," I said immediately, reaching for my phone.

"Moretti, wait. Before you go commando, hear me out," Colleen insisted, grabbing my hand to stop me. "I've hacked into this chick's personal information. Let me tell you everything before you do anything."

"Colleen, you don't understand," I argued, yanking my hand from her. "Lexi is with Paige constantly for work. She could be in danger right now. I have to tell someone."

"Relax. She's at Panera with your brother." She rolled her eyes, the words making mine go wide. "What? You think I didn't put a tracker on her? Give me some credit."

"Look, I don't know anything about the secret squirrel spy shit you've got going on, but you should have gone to campus security months ago. If she's in danger, she needs to know now."

"Good God, don't you ever listen? You're the most annoying person I've ever met. I should have just called your brother instead. He's less annoying and would actually listen to me instead of arguing." She shook her head. "I don't know why I thought you would listen. First of all, I can't go to the police, dumb ass. If word got out about what I do here, it would be a disaster. What you need to do is show this video to your brother and confirm it's her car, then go to the police and pressure them to bring her in for questioning. You *must* keep my identity a secret. I know I am asking a lot here; we are not friends. But this is the deal, take it or leave it. I'll give you what I have to help your friend, but you have to promise to keep your mouth shut about where it came from."

"I promise," I said immediately. "I'll take it to the grave, but you have to promise me something in return. If you find out Lexi's in trouble, you'll call the police and then us."

"Moretti, I may be an asshole, but I do have a heart," she said, standing to leave. "Why the fuck to do you think I tortured myself by talking to you today? Obviously, I'll call if she's in trouble."

"Thank you. I owe you one, and I swear I won't tell anyone," I said, offering a small smile of gratitude. "I have a lot of respect for people who tell it like it is. I really think we could have been friends if things were different."

I felt guilty for all the times I'd been a dick to her, not that she'd made it easy on me. I was struggling with whether I should hug her or shake her hand, but she made it easy by simply nodding at me and walking away.

Within seconds, the video was on my phone, and I called Frankie.

"What's up?"

"I need you to come and get me, Frankie. I know something that will help Lexi's case."

"Are you fucking kidding me?" he railed as he looked at the video, instantly recognizing Paige's car before his eyes moved to Lexi, his expression riddled with guilt. "I brought her right to your fucking door, Lexi. You were almost killed because of me."

"No, you will *not* blame yourself for this, Frankie." She shook her head immediately. "You had no idea she was unstable."

"It doesn't matter, baby. None of this shit would have ever happened to you if it wasn't for me."

"Stop it," she insisted. "You're not going to take what we have and allow her to dirty it."

"She's right," I agreed. "None of us knew what a nut job she was."

"Where did you get this?" he asked, staring back down at my phone.

"I don't know," I lied, hoping it held up. "I got a text from an unknown number, and that was all they sent."

"This must be the same person who sent it to the police," Lexi said.

"We have to talk to Walsh. I don't want that bitch walking the street any longer," Frankie said, ushering us to his truck.

When we arrived at the station, we were told that they'd tried calling her in for questioning, and she hadn't returned their calls. That's all it took for Frankie to lose it.

"No shit, she isn't calling you," he yelled across Officer Walsh's desk. "She is a criminal. Why would she?"

"Mr. Moretti, this is the last time I will warn you about your outbursts." He glared back.

"Well, do something! Help her!"

"We are," Walsh insisted, composing himself before he continued. "Ms. Cole is safe. We've had eyes on her since the incident to ensure she's protected."

"Wait, I'm being followed?" Lexi asked.

"Yes," he confessed. "Your father hired a security person to keep an eye on you before you ever left the hospital, Ms. Cole. Ms. Matthews is a person of interest. However, until we can interview her, there's little else we can do with the evidence we have. In the meantime, if you come in contact with her in any way, contact us immediately."

As we left the police station, Frankie was beside himself while Lexi was silent.

"This is bullshit," he finally said as we got back into his truck. "Lexi, you're not leaving my fucking sight until that crazy bitch is in jail. Call your dad and let him know what is going on. Gia, call Mikey and Joey. I want a fucking security company at the brownstone within the hour to install a system that Houdini himself couldn't fucking breakthrough."

"Frankie, please calm down," Lexi whispered as she looked over at him. "You're scaring me."

"Lexi, this shit ends today. If I can't choke the bitch out myself without going to prison, you gotta let me handle it."

"Okay, fine," she said, putting her hands up in surrender. "But you can't be with me twenty-four hours a day, Frankie. I have school."

"We'll email your professors so that you can do it online for now." He sighed, glancing into the rearview to meet my eyes. "Gia when you get back from Thanksgiving break, you and Shelby are doing the same thing. I don't trust her not going after you to get back at me."

"Frankie, don't you think you're going a bit overboard right now locking us down?" I asked, shaking my head.

"Gia, when it comes to keeping you safe, I don't care how far I have to go." He stared back at me, his jaw tense. "Now for once, can you just do what the fuck I say, please?"

155

I held his gaze for a second, swallowing hard as I saw the fear flashing in his eyes before giving him a subtle nod.

"I'll call the guys now," I promised, filling them in when they answered. As we suspected, they hadn't heard anything from Paige, either.

As we pulled up to my mom's a few minutes later, Frankie threw the truck into park and followed us in, his chest raging as he slammed the door shut and stormed upstairs, leaving Lexi and I standing in the entryway.

"I know he loves me, Gia, but he has a really shitty way of showing it sometimes," Lexi said low, sniffing her tears back.

"He's just pissed off right now, Lexi. I know my brother. Give him a minute, and he will get a grip," I said reaching for her hand. "Until then, call your dad and fill him in, okay?"

She pulled out her phone and dialed her father, giving him a quick recap before finally asking him about the security he'd hired to follow her.

"He's a friend of mine, a retired private investigator who lives in the area and owed me a favor," he explained. "I know you're probably upset, but I couldn't leave you without protection, Lexi."

"I'm not mad, Daddy. I just wish you'd told me."

"Honey, if I had, you would have spent your time looking for him and not focusing on getting your life back," he reasoned. "He was there to keep you safe, not suffocate you."

"Thank you, Daddy," she said, wiping the tear from her cheek. "Please no more secrets. It's just us now. All we have is honesty" Lexi said letting a tear slip down her cheek.

"I promise," he replied. "Is Frankie there? I'd like to speak to him."

"He's upstairs. I'm sure he'll call you once he calms down. He's just really upset right now."

"Understood." He sighed. "Please have him call me as soon as possible. We all need to be on the same page to keep you safe. I love you."

"I will," she promised. "Thank you, Daddy. Please don't worry. I'm going to be fine. I love you, too."

She hung up her phone, slipping it back into her purse before releasing a long sigh and looking at me again.

"I'm sorry you and Shelby are getting pulled into this," she offered. "Maybe once Frankie calms down, we'll realize he's overreacting, and we can come to some kind of compromise."

"Lexi, you have to stop downplaying this shit," I insisted. "We're all in this together, and we'll figure it out. The important thing is that we're all safe."

Shelby was the only one left who didn't know what was going on, but Joey was meeting her at the stables once her shift was over, so we knew she'd be safe. When she arrived later that evening, her expression made it clear that Joey had filled her in on the ride over.

"Are you okay?" she asked, immediately making her way over to Lexi and pulling her close.

"I'm fine," Lexi promised, pulling away to face her. "We don't even know for sure it was Paige driving. I know it seems fishy, but I've been alone with her dozens of times since, and she's never been aggressive."

"It doesn't matter Lexi," Frankie interjected. "In some cases, they just need a trigger, and then it's all over. Thank God there wasn't one to set her off."

Craig

Where the fuck is she?

I had been calling her cell phone for two days, and nothing. I knew this chick was a few cents short of a dollar, but she was the closest thing I had to Lexi, and if I had to endure screwing her brains out to get what I wanted, then so be it.

After Lexi was attacked, I was brought in for questioning and finally released. Paige reached out to me sympathetically as one scorned lover to another. She cried over losing Frankie to Lexi and how we both had been dealt a shitty hand. It might have made me an asshole, but I saw an opportunity. As long as this bitch still had a working relationship with that moron, I could keep tabs on Lexi and get laid at the same time.

I left her another message and tossed my phone to the side in annoyance. If I didn't hear back from her by the next morning, I'd have to pay her a little visit and teach her some manners.

Why did all the good fucks have to be such a pain in the ass?

Gia

After an hour of listening to everyone banter back and forth on what we should do, I glanced over to find Lexi getting overwhelmed at the testosterone filling the room.

"Listen, we get that you're worried about our safety, but you can't just lock us up in a house until they speak to Paige. It's stupid," I insisted, my hand going up to keep Frankie quiet when he started to disagree. "We share most of the same classes and even considering the ones we don't, we're never more than two buildings away from each other. Lexi already has a PI following her, which means the guy has eyes on us as well. The only time we're apart is when Shelby's at work, but she's leaving for break and will be safe in Montana. Both of us will be with you and Colin for the next week, so why can't we just save this for when we all get back? It'll give us time to talk to Lexi's father and come to a rational agreement that doesn't have this steamrolling our lives, Frankie," I said in a huff. "Besides, you're stressing me the fuck out, never mind what you're doing to Lexi."

"Gia has a point," Ma said, giving them *the look*. "We can't let this rule our lives, and you're doing all you can to keep them safe."

"I am sorry if everyone thinks I am overreacting," Frankie said with a sigh, pulling Lexi into his lap. "I definitely don't want to scare you, honey, but this is serious shit. Once your dad gets here, we will come up with something more reasonable, but for now, you're just going to have to deal with me being your shadow."

"Okay," she sighed, giving Frankie a quick kiss before leaning against him in exhaustion. "I'm sorry I've brought all of this to you. I know none of us knew Paige was crazy, but you shouldn't have to stop and deal with all this crap."

Nonna, who had been sitting listening to everyone, finally piped in. "Lexi, this girl is *lei è pazza*," Nonna said, tapping her head as she stood from the table and moved toward her bedroom. "It's no one's fault. Move on."

She was right. It was time to move on.

The next few days were uneventful. We were either at the apartment or my mom's house while Frankie kept in touch with the police daily and left Paige messages with no response. Even her boss said she hadn't checked in or called in almost a week.

Frankie was true to his word, only letting Lexi out of his sight when the poor kid went to the bathroom. The security system he had installed that first day was insane, but we knew we were safe.

In a few short hours, Colin would finally be back in Boston. God, I'd missed him. Christian was due to pick Shelby up any minute so that they could head to Montana. His long-distance romance with her sister, Sara, gave me hope for things with Colin. The sound of a horn honking pulled me from my thoughts as Shelby returned to the living room.

"Alright, girls. My ride is here," she announced, pulling us both close for a hug. "Wish me luck."

"Have fun and enjoy the time with your family," Lexi smiled. "And try and give Jake a chance. You deserve to be happy, too."

"I will try," she promised, moving closer to the door. "Keep me posted on what is going on."

"You got it, cowgirl." I winked, slapping her ass just in time for her to open the door to Christian. "Now giddy-up on outta here."

"Hey, ladies." He grinned, giving us each a hug. "How've you been?"

"All good here, Rodeo Rick." I smiled. "You take care of our little cowpoke and make sure she has a good time. Oh, and be kind to Jake. He is new to all this ranch shit. We don't want to scare him off with the all the poop and animal things out there."

"No worries." He laughed. "I know what it's like to be the new guy. I've got his back." He grabbed Shelby's bag and headed downstairs. "Alright, we take off in less than two hours. Let's get rolling."

As she turned to give us a final wave, the nerves were all over her face, but we were happy for her.

She needed to step out of her comfort zone, and Jake was just the guy to help her do that.

Chapter Ten

Gia

By the time Colin texted me to say he was in a cab and on his way from the airport, I was nearly jumping from my skin with excitement. I couldn't stand sitting in the house a second longer, so I walked outside to wait for him on the steps, the memory of me waiting for my father like this as a child making me sad. Before the feeling could overtake me, my phone buzzed, and I felt my lips moving into a wide smile.

It was Colin.

> **On my way, baby! Can't wait to see you. I'll be there in less than five**
>
> *Hurry up! I miss you!*
>
> **That's my girl.**

My heart sped up. I was smiling like a dork when I heard an annoying voice coming from next door.

"Hello, Georgia." Samantha smirked as she walked down her steps looking down at her phone.

"Afternoon, Sally," I replied, giving her my best fake smile.

"It's Samantha."

"You say tomato, I say tomahto." I shrugged, standing to brush off my pants. I was about to walk back inside when Colin's cab pulled up, and he stepped onto the sidewalk.

"Gia, you'd best get your ass down here and give me some lovin'," he warned playfully, making me smile wide.

As I bounded down the steps toward him, Samantha stood in shock, already forgotten as I wrapped myself around him. I kissed him long and hard until the cab driver honked for his money. Colin laughed when I refused to release him as he dug into his pocket and pulled out a fifty.

"Thanks, buddy," he said, paying the driver. "Keep the change."

The cab was about to pull away when Samantha slithered over, batting her eyelashes at Colin.

"Would you mind if I took your cab?" she asked, her voice dripping with enough sweetness to make me sick. "I've got to go into the city. It'd sure help me out."

"Have at it," he shrugged, burying his face in my neck, ignoring her as he showered me with kisses. "I'm not going anywhere for a while."

"Great, thank you." She smiled, flipping her hair. "I'm Samantha, by the way."

Colin never took his attention off of me as she turned toward the cab.

"Enjoy the ride, Sara," I called back childishly. "I know I will."

Frankie and Lexi were shopping with my mom, and Shelby was already halfway to Montana, so when we finally stepped inside, we were all alone. He dropped his bags in the entryway and immediately, his lips were on mine, nipping and sucking his way down my neck.

"Do I want to know what's going on with you and your neighbor?" he asked, his voice husky.

"N-no," I stammered, my head falling against the wall behind me. "She's just a dickface."

"Oh, okay." He smirked, moving lower. "My dick's been hard since I boarded the plane this morning," Colin confessed, nuzzling into my neck before sinking his lips into my breasts. "I had to keep my coat over my pants, so the good senator didn't get a peek at my boy trying to stick his head out."

"I am sure Cynthia would have gotten an eye full as well," I said with a breathy laugh.

"Hmm, less talking," he said as I pulled my shirt over my head and dropped it onto the floor. "Where is your room?"

"Upstairs. No one else is home right now."

"Good, because I am about to make you see fucking stars."

Before I could respond, he threw me over his shoulder and took the stairs like Rocky, kicking my door open before returning me to my feet and kissing me feverishly. He led me to my bed, his lips never slowing as he lowered us both and rested between my thighs, hovering over me silently as he stared down at me.

"What's wrong?" I asked, growing insecure. "Did you change your mind?"

I began to look away when his finger caught my chin and pulled my eyes back to his.

"Look at me," he demanded gently. "Don't ever take your eyes off me when we're together. I want you looking at me the whole time."

I nodded, cursing the silent tear that slid down my cheek as he leaned in to kiss me, stopping when he noticed.

"Why, the tears baby?" he asked as he licked it away.

"I just don't know how to respond to you sometimes," I admitted, my cheeks red with embarrassment. "You always say all this nice shit to me, but I'm not used to guys treating me like you do."

"Well, I'm not a boy, Gia. I'm a man," he corrected, grabbing my chin once more and pulling my gaze back. "Eyes."

"Bossy much?" I teased, twisting my hips to relieve the ache building between my thighs.

He groaned and kissed me hard until I felt like I would melt straight into the mattress. When he pulled away a few moments later, he kicked his shoes off while I leaned up on my elbows to watch him undress. I moved to unzip my jeans, but he pushed my hands away.

"No, ma'am." He tsked. "This is like an early Christmas present, and we're about to unwrap each section slowly so I can enjoy it."

He stepped closer, toward the edge of the bed, staring down at me as his length saluted me proudly, making my mouth go dry.

"Take off your bra," he ordered softly, pleased when the lace fell onto the floor.

His fingers reached for the waist of my jeans, slowly unbuckling them before pulling them off in one swift motion. *So much for patience*, I thought as he ripped the metaphoric wrapping paper away in haste. My thoughts had me smirking to

165

myself, but in the next movement, his fingers hooked beneath my lace thong and ripped it away abruptly, leaving me naked.

"Those were my favorite, and they weren't cheap!" I exclaimed, making him smirk.

"I'll take you shopping to replace what I've ruined," he husked against my lips. "I promise that won't be the last pair. Now hush, Gia."

"Okay," I managed, frazzled and more turned on than I'd ever been before. "Come on, baby. I'm dying over here."

He took his time as he pushed into me, my back arching lifting my hips just enough to pull him in deeper and make me gasp.

"Are you okay?" he asked, his eyes heavy with lust. "Do you want me to stop?"

"If you stop right now, I'll punch you in the face," I gasped, gripping his ass and pulling him into me all at once.

"Gia, fuck," he groaned with pleasure.

Slowly, we found the rhythm, his hot breath falling on my chest pushing us both to the edge. We climbed high together, dangerously close to climax when we heard the front door swing open downstairs, the voice that could make any dick go limp trailing after it.

"Gia? Honey, are you here?" she called out, making my eyes go wide. "This girl is such a slob. Look! She just left her shirt laying in the middle of the floor."

"Gia, we are all here to see you," Frankie shouted, his voice dripping with sarcasm. "Come on down."

"Frankie, stop being an ass," Lexi admonished him. "You know Colin just got here. I bet you did this on purpose."

"Oh, my God!" I whispered up at Colin, both of us frozen in place. "What do we do?"

"How the hell should I know? She's your mother. Right now, I am balls deep in her daughter." Colin panicked, pulling out and honestly, leaving me to feel like what we'd done was dirty. "This isn't going to go well for either of us."

He reached for his clothes, dressing faster than anyone I'd ever seen, and as I rose from the mattress, I covered myself with embarrassment as I did the same. Frankie stomped up the stairs, his fingers tapping on the door just as I pulled a shirt over myself and released a low breath of relief.

"Gia? Colin?" he sang with a chuckle. "Everything okay in there?"

"Yes, you can come in."

Opening the door slowly, he had his eyes closed and his hand over Lexi's eyes as if they were going to see tits and ass everywhere.

"Are you descent, little sister?"

"We're not naked, stupid. We were just talking." I rolled my eyes, elbowing Colin when I saw his cat-who-ate-the-canary grin. "Where's Ma?"

Opening his eyes and releasing Lexi, he looked for signs of sex and thankfully, found none.

"She's downstairs putting food away," he said, leaning against the doorway. "I didn't want her to come up here and find her daughter nailing my business partner."

"Stop it." Lexi swatted at him. "You're embarrassing them."

"Don't show Gia any pity, babe. She's cockblocked me so many times." He pointed at me accusingly. "This is just a little payback."

"How was your flight, Colin?" Lexi asked.

167

"There was a little turbulence, but I still found it to be quite enjoyable," he said, winking at me.

"Well, I'm going downstairs to see Ma," I said, lifting from the bed and pushing past them.

"Hey, Gia?" Lexi stopped me, her voice low as her cheeks flamed. "You have a thong stuck to your shirt... which is also inside out."

"Busted." Frankie laughed.

"I am *this close* to kicking you in the nuts," I warned, pushing past him to go downstairs as Colin followed me out.

"Next time, why not help a brother out and shoot me a text?" Colin asked, punching him in the arm. "That could have been disastrous."

"Punch me like that again, and you'll see a real disaster because you'll be picking your teeth up off the floor."

"Would you two stop it? Gia is completely mortified right now," Lexi said, shoving them both out. "Get downstairs and act like gentlemen."

We settled in the kitchen, discussing everything from vacation to Paige, to the food we would be eating the next day at Casa Moretti. When Lexi's phone rang, our eyes all turned to find her staring down at her phone nervously.

"It's the police department," she said quietly, putting the phone on speaker before answering. "Hello?"

"Ms. Cole, this is Officer Walsh."

"Hi Officer Walsh," she answered politely. "What can I do for you?"

"I wanted to inform you that we obtained a search warrant for Ms. Matthews' apartment this morning, and when we entered it with her landlord, it was empty. As of right now, her whereabouts are unknown, but we're still looking. I wanted to keep you abreast of our findings."

"What do you mean, it was empty?" Frankie bellowed.

"Frankie, calm down right now," Ma said grabbing his arm.

"Cleaned out," Walsh reiterated. "The only thing left inside was a check for the landlord to cover her last month's rent and the penalty for breaking the lease."

"This is bullshit. No one vanishes into thin air," Frankie fumed. "Have any of your crackerjack cops tried checking her credit cards?"

"We're doing all we can to try and locate her by all means necessary, sir. We wanted to let you know and will continue to keep you updated," Walsh said, his voice exhausted. "Ms. Cole, I have a meeting in an hour to brief your father and your private security."

I listened as they finished the call, an idea popping into my head. Since Colleen was able to hack into Paige's shit, it stood to reason she might be able to help me find out where she was hiding. I knew what the police didn't, but I also knew contacting her was almost as bad as giving her name up myself.

I scrolled through my phone, wracking my brain when I found her school email and another lightbulb went off. As I quickly tapped the keys on my phone, I just hoped she didn't ignore me.

Hey Roomie,

Miss me yet? Please give me a call when you get this. I seem to be missing a few things and need your help locating them as soon as possible.

Thanks,

Gia

Lexi

It took Theresa, Colin, and a phone call to my father to finally pull Frankie off the ledge after talking to Officer Walsh. I moved toward the front window, wrapping my arms around myself for some semblance of security, but finding little as I stared into the night. I searched the street, the sight of a dark sports car with tinted windows catching my notice only seconds before it sped away. I brushed off my paranoid thoughts, silently returning them to the case and hoping that they'd figure it out quickly. Frankie's arms fell around my waist, pulling me close to his chest.

"I'm sorry, baby," he whispered in my ear, kissing my temple. "Please don't be mad at me for loving you. I just want to protect you."

"I know." I nodded, turning to face him as I rested my hand on his jaw. "I'm not mad at you. I understand, but you just have to keep your temper in check. It scares the hell out of me sometimes," I admitted. "I know you don't mean it towards me, but I can't have the man I love most slamming his fist into everything in sight every time something doesn't go his way."

"I know," he sighed, returning my kiss and holding me close as I rested my cheek against his chest. "I'll try to be better. I can't guarantee any miracles, but I'll try baby," he promised.

Chapter Eleven

Lexi

When we went to Frankie's house to meet my father, I was nervous he'd react even more defensively after his meeting with Officer Walsh. Instead, I was surprised to find him sidled up to the island in the kitchen with Angus, Nonna, and Cynthia, eating lunch. When he heard me walk in, he turned to greet me with a smile.

"Baby girl." He beamed. "Come here. I've missed you."

"Hi, Daddy." I smiled, kissing his cheek. "I've missed you, too. I'm so glad you came."

"What about me, lass?" Angus pouted playfully, making Mama giggle behind me. "I'm a lonely old man, too."

"Good Lord, Theresa. You are like a little school girl for Christ's sake," Nonna teased. "Am I done here, boys? I have a television to yell at."

"Lexi, have a seat." My father gestured toward the empty stool beside him. "We need to catch you up."

He better explained the private investigator he'd hired and told me they'd be stepping up security since Paige was on the run. I personally thought it was overkill—she'd had plenty of chances to take me out if it was what she truly wanted—but it made them feel better, so I didn't argue. The next day we'd be celebrating Thanksgiving, so Theresa ordered us all out once we finished talking. Needing an easy night desperately, we decided to go to the bonfire like we had the year before. My father, Angus, and Cynthia stayed behind to help Theresa prepare the feast, and I loved seeing her smiling so much.

As for my father and Cynthia, they'd been a well-oiled machine for years, and I knew he trusted her completely, not just with his career, but his life. I could never condone adultery, but I knew my father had his reasons and did what he thought was best for me, regardless of the vows he'd taken with my mother. As hateful as she'd been to me my whole life, I couldn't imagine the hell she'd put him through. I was in no position to judge him for anything.

"You okay, baby?" Frankie asked, squeezing my hand as he parked at the school.

"Yes, just thinking about my dad and Cynthia."

"I hear you," he sighed. "I am thinking about Angus and my mother," he admitted, glancing back at Colin. "What the fuck is up with that shit?"

"Dude, I'm not my father's keeper, and you're not your mother's. As long as they're happy, who are we to stand in their way?"

"He's right, Frankie. Ma has been alone for over seven years, not one single date. She's always taking care of Nonna and us and never does anything for herself. Let her live her life," Gia said, reaching for Colin's hand and leading him toward the crowd.

"Right, my ass," he grumbled. "I don't want to have to deal with the bullshit when Angus dumps her ass and leaves her heartbroken. I am still waiting for Colin to get sick of Gia and for that shit storm to hit."

"Frankie, stop."

"What, Lexi? You know I'm right." He shrugged. "Haven't you ever heard that saying, *don't shit where you eat?*"

"Yes, and if that applies to our parents, I guess you have a seat at the same buffet as I do." I shook my head. "You can't act like a control freak, dictating who likes each other, Frankie. What gives you the right to—"

"My father cheating on my mother and then dying, leaving her to take care of two fucking kids while I couldn't do shit to help her. That's what gives me the right, Lex."

His words shocked me. I'd never heard him say an ill word about his father, but one look at his expression proved there was a crack in the Moretti foundation.

"Frankie, I had no idea."

"No one does," he whispered, clearing his throat. "My mom stood by him, knowing that he was fucking around, and held her head high until he died. After that, she was broken beyond repair. I vowed then I'd never let that happen to her again," he admitted, glancing over at me. "So, I'm sorry if that makes me a control freak, but now you know why I am the way I am."

"My dad did the same thing to my mother," I said, grabbing his hand. "Did he break her?"

"Babe, you know that story better than me, but I think it's safe to say that was different. Your mother stopped loving your father, but he still gave her all he had knowing he'd get nothing in return, not even a way out. He had every right," Frankie said.

"My dad was loved and taken care of, but he still chose to dip his dick elsewhere. My mother was the perfect wife and mother to all of us. When she asked him why he told her living with someone so perfect made him feel imperfect." He shook his head. "What a line of bullshit. How do you shit all over a woman like that? I never stopped loving him, but my respect for him was gone. That's why I went to work at Castagna after he died so I could show my mother she did it right and raised a real man."

"I can't imagine how hard that was to go through, but if your mother can find happiness with Angus or anyone else for that matter, you need to let her," I insisted. "She needs to be happy."

His eyes found mine, and he reluctantly gave me a gentle nod, kissing my hair.

"I'm not my dad," he promised. "Don't ever doubt that you're all I've ever wanted. I love you, Lexi."

"I love you, too." I returned his kiss before tugging him forward. "Now, come on. I'm freezing."

"Fine, bossy." He chuckled. "But when we get home, I'm reminding you of who's in charge."

Craig

I sipped my whiskey at the Stanza Dei Sigari on the north end of town, glancing down at my phone in annoyance. I still hadn't heard shit from Paige, and it was really starting to piss me off. I pulled her number up and typed in another message, tossing my phone onto the bar.

Where the fuck are you?

My mind began to wander back to how all this started, and I picked up my phone again, this time sending Alexis a text I knew she wouldn't reply to. Why not? It'd been a while since I'd ruined her night.

> **Happy Thanksgiving. Give my best to your asshole boyfriend. Or not. I don't give a shit. I am sure I will see you both soon.**

I hit send and smiled. Fuck them both. They thought their shit didn't stink, but someday, I would show her just how right her mother was. She needed a man to put her in her place and keep her there, not that Guido pussy she'd been fucking.

My phone vibrated, surprising me as I glanced down at the message from the unknown number.

> *You lied to me. You never wanted to be with me. You used me to get to that slut. Fuck you!*

That had to be Paige. Who else could it be? Dumb bitch. When I got my hands on her, she'd regret fucking with me.

A hand sliding down the front of my shirt pulled me back once more, and I glanced over my shoulder to find Kerrie, my father's top account manager at the office. I'd had my eye on her for a while, but I'd been told to keep my hands off her. However, when Daddy was away…

Her hand slid lower to my thigh as she took a seat beside me, talking to the rest of the group like it was nothing. *Easy prey*, I thought as I leaned in, gesturing for her to come closer.

"If you are going to put your hand on my leg, you'd better be prepared to put those pouty lips around my dick as well," I husked into her ear before taking a pull from my Monte Cristo cigar, the smoke floating over my head.

My bold statement made her lick her whore lips and smile. She needed to be taught a lesson and would choke on my dick for being so forward. As for Paige, she'd regret that last text message. This night just kept getting better and better.

I didn't want her at my place, so I made her get on her knees in the fucking alley to blow me. It was cold as fuck, but my dick didn't care. Besides, if she wanted to act like a whore, she'd be treated as such. She took my dick like a trooper, never stopping until I pulled her head away. I thought she wasn't bad and would do in a pinch, but her smart mouth killed my vibe.

"Hey, what about me?" she whined.

"You have fingers." I shrugged, zipping my pants. "Have at it."

I stepped away from her, heading back inside without a second glance when I heard her again.

"You're a fucking prick."

I turned around and reached her in three quick steps, grabbing her by the throat before pressing her against the brick wall beside us. "You're right. I am a fucking prick. Remember it the next time you think you can manipulate me," I spat. "Now, keep your fucking mouth shut. Fuck with me again, and I'll ruin you. The last thing you want is the owner's son filing a fucking sexual harassment charge against you." I released her roughly, seeing the finger marks already on her skin as she stumbled back. "Am I clear?"

"Yes," she said, gasping for air and bending over to catch her breath.

"Get the fuck out of here," I said, flexing my fist. "I'm done with you."

Lexi

We were standing around the fire when I felt my phone vibrate. When I saw it was a text from Craig, my stomach began to knot. The last thing I wanted was to ruin what had turned out to be a fun night, but I knew keeping it from Frankie would be a mistake, so I thought better of it, interrupting his conversation with Mikey.

"What's up, babe?" he asked, taking it from my hand. "Are you kidding me? That miserable little prick has got to have the biggest set of balls." He shook his head, furious as he showed Gia and the guys the text, sparking their own reactions. "Come on, babe. Grab your shit. We're leaving."

"Frankie, please don't do anything stupid," I begged. "He just wants you to retaliate so he can press charges. I know him. He loves to goad people on and then strike.

"I'll let your father handle it, babe," he promised. "Besides, I know enough people in this town that his bullshit charges would never stick."

The ride home was silent, which only made me more nervous, knowing Frankie was thinking about how to go after Craig. When we walked inside, he went straight to my father, who was helping make pies.

"Jackson," he started, handing him my phone. "Look at this fuckin' text."

"Whoa, there son," Angus said, rounding the corner. "What's climbed up your ass?"

"Are you okay, honey?" my dad asked, pulling a nod from me before looking down at the screen. "I'll forward this to Officer Walsh. In the meantime, Frankie, please keep your wits about you. This little shit only wants a reaction out of you, and so far, he seems to be succeeding," he said bluntly before glancing toward Theresa. "Would it be all right if the girls stayed here tonight? I don't trust him to leave them alone."

"Yes, of course," Theresa said, hugging me close. "I would feel much better knowing everyone is under one roof."

Gia

It was a universal truth that just when you thought things were going great, something always shit all over it.

Since we had to stay at my mother's house, I had no idea how Colin and I would be able to finish what we started back at the brownstone. I felt cursed like my vagina had one of those circle things with a slash through it. *Do Not Enter*, it warned, while I just wanted to scream. I'd hoped Colin would side with me, but of course, he agreed with my mother and wanted me safe. *Jackass.* I hoped his balls exploded from lack of use.

I gave my best pouty face until he promised we'd fool around after everyone went to bed, but since we were under my mother's roof, he refused to have sex with me.

We'll see about that, I thought. If nothing else, I was getting an orgasm out of him. After the humiliation I'd endured that afternoon with my brother and the way he'd been teasing me all afternoon, it was the least he could do.

Watching my mother flirt with Angus was awkward. She was flipping her hair, swaying her hips, giggling—she was a mess. I'd have to sit her down and give her some lessons. At least Angus was just as interested in her. It was apparent by the way he kept touching her arm while they cooked, laughed at her jokes, and stayed attentive. Even though it was my mother, it was still cute. She'd never brought a man home, never mind let one in her kitchen. When I glanced over at Frankie, not just still pissed about Craig, but now giving Angus the stink eye, I couldn't help but laugh as I nudged Colin.

"What's so funny you two?" Ma asked, turning away from the ravioli.

"Nothing, Ma," I lied, flashing her a smile. "Colin is just acting like a dork."

"Frankie?" Nonna yelled as she moved through the kitchen. "Why do you look constipated?"

"I'm fine," he insisted, standing to give her his seat.

"Bullshit," she said, smacking him with her cane. "You look like you've got a lemon up your ass. Stop ruining your handsome face."

Colin's laughter rolled through the kitchen, only further irritating Frankie.

"Cut the shit and stop being a dick," Frankie snapped.

After a few more rounds, Ma had had enough, slamming her spoon onto the counter.

"All right, why don't you both cut the shit?" She raised her eyebrow. "Boys, get the tables and chairs set up. Lexi, go help your father and Cynthia put things in the fridge down in the cellar."

I was grateful to have gotten out of helping until I saw Nonna going in for the kill, dipping a clean spoon into the ravioli filling Ma was working on and giving it a taste. "Needs more pecorino," she said bluntly. "It has no flavor."

"Stubborn old broad," Ma mumbled, obviously pissed. "It tastes fine."

"I may be old, Theresa, but I am not deaf," Nonna snipped as she walked away. "You need to add more cheese. Otherwise, they are going to taste like shit."

"I may not be Italian," Angus said as he tasted it for himself and gently tapped his spoon to her nose. "But it tastes awesome to me."

"Ma, where do you want these?" Frankie asked, the tables falling hard enough against the floor to make us jump.

"Frankie, I said to put them in the living room." She ignored his innocent look as she added more cheese to the filling. "Next time, listen."

"Shit, these are heavy," Colin said, trying to push past him. "Move."

"Gia, get your ass in there and wipe all the stuff down," she ordered, cutting my laughter short as she tossed a wet towel at me.

I slid from my seat and waited for Frankie to get everything set up before I started cleaning everything, the feel of Colin's hand low on my waist making me crazy.

"If we were alone, I would bend you over that table and have my own Thanksgiving feast," he husked, smacking my ass.

"Tease," I replied.

"Don't worry." He winked. "I'll take care of you later."

Lexi

Watching my father with Cynthia made my heart swell.

There was a part of me that felt like I might be disrespecting my mother by supporting my father's relationship with Cynthia, but I quickly brushed the thought away. My mother had brought that all on herself, and Cynthia had always treated me with respect. I decided it was time to get to know her better and pulled up a chair beside her to help with the charcuterie platter she was working on.

"This is almost too beautiful to eat." I smiled at her.

"Thank you, Alexis," she replied, returning my smile. "When we would have family parties, this would be one of the main appetizers. Everyone seemed to love it, so I thought I would do one for tomorrow."

"Is your family spending the holiday in Washington?"

"No, I was an only child and lost my parents years ago," she admitted. "Usually, my Thanksgivings are spent alone, eating a turkey dinner from Whole Foods."

"Well, now you have a new tradition," I reassured her, "spending it with us."

My father made his way over with a warm smile, giving each of us a kiss on the cheek.

"It's nice to see the two women who have been the best part of my life getting along." He beamed, glancing over at Angus after a moment. "Hey, old man. Why don't you grab that bourbon I brought up with me and let the ladies finish?"

"Sounds good," he answered, playfully bumping Theresa's hip with his own. "Let me just finish helping with this, and I'll be outside to have a cigar with you."

"Go," she waved him off. "You've done more than enough to help. You deserve a break."

"Jesus Christ." He chuckled as she shoved him toward the door. "Talk about getting rid of me."

"Just tell me how," Frankie grumbled under his breath, my father and Colin laughing as they followed him out.

Theresa

Spending time with Angus made me feel young again.

After Gino died, I never dated. I didn't want to bring another man into my children's life out of respect for their father's memory. They suffered enough losing him at such a young age. But now, they were grown, and I was done being alone.

Besides, I never had someone pay attention to just *me*. I had no idea where this whole thing with Angus would take me, but I was ready to live my life and have some fun. I felt like he was the right man for the job.

"Ma!" Gia shouted, pulling me from my thoughts. "You want to come back to earth over there? I need more ravs to fork."

"Sorry, I was just thinking how wonderful it is having all of you home."

"Yeah?" she teased. "You sure you're not thinking about Angus' tight ass?"

"I know I was," Nonna yelled from her room, making my face go red.

"Oh, my God!" I swatted at them with my towel. "You people are out of control. Lexi, save me please."

"Sorry, Theresa, but I have to agree with Nonna." She shrugged. "That's a mighty fine ass."

"Theresa, it's okay. Don't be embarrassed. You two make a cute couple," Cynthia piped in.

Trying to keep my flushed face at bay, I started to fan myself.

"Okay, Gia. Block your ears," I said, watching her roll her eyes instead. "He is hot, and I get all stupid around him, but he must have women who are much prettier and more sophisticated than me falling all over him in Charleston."

"Nope." Gia smiled. "According to Colin, he hasn't dated seriously, has never brought a woman home, and look, he has already invited us down for New Year's."

Thinking back on it, he did mention he would love to have us down to Charleston for the holidays. Unfortunately, we have too many people here on Christmas Eve to up and leave, but New Years could be fun.

Angus

It was cold as hell sitting outside, smoking our cigars, but the bourbon warmed us right up. There was something about a fire pit and guys. We just had to see how big we could get the flames before the fire department showed up. This one was roaring and throwing some heat, taking a bit of the chill away. Swirling my cigar in the amber liquid, I inhaled, releasing the smoke while enjoying the mixed flavor. That was when I decided to open a can of worms.

"Frankie, I would like to ask your permission while I am here to take your mother out to dinner."

"Why are you asking me? You should be asking her," he snipped.

"I already did, but it seems you have a bit of a problem with me showing any interest in your mother, so I thought I would ask for your blessing. I don't want us to have any beef," I admitted, taking another pull off my cigar, lifting my chin while the smoke swirled from my mouth, challenging him to say something.

"No beef here, Angus. I'll tell you the same thing I told your son when he started to date Gia. If you hurt her, I will make you regret the day you met me. That I can fucking promise. Are we clear?" Frankie said, leaning forward to make his point.

"We are." I nodded.

"Okay, if you boys are ready to put your cocks away..." Colin said throwing another log on the already growing fire.

"Yeah, you two are ruining the ambiance with all this tough guy bullshit." Jackson laughed.

"Oh, look who's talking." I chuckled, kicking his chair. "You want to fill us in on the story with you and Cynthia?"

"It's none of your business." Jackson smirked. "How's that grab your ass?"

"Fine." I shrugged, filling my glass. "Don't throw shit if you can't take the stink."

"Give me the bourbon." He swiped it from me as I laughed.

"Vaginas," Colin chuckled. "You're all vaginas."

Shelby

Waiting for Jake and Campbelle to arrive was torture, and it didn't help that my sisters were annoying me with a million questions about them. Desperate to clear my head, I decided to take Dancer for a ride, knowing he was the only thing that would calm my frazzled nerves. As soon as I was in the saddle, it was like he knew where to go and took off at a trot before gracefully moving into a full gallop, crossing the field and heading toward the path that would take us to the waterfall, where I could relax until they arrived.

Once we got to the falls, I hopped off and let him graze on the dewy grass while I went to the rock Drew and I would sit on when we came here. I sat and just watched the ripples from the cascading water dance against the stones.

I was resting my head on my knees. Emotions I'd fought for years bubbled up once more at the thought of Drew, wreaking havoc as tears began to threaten. I glanced up at the sky and released a low breath, composing myself when I saw movement in front of me, pulling my eyes down to find the cardinal landing nearby. I gasped. My hopes of holding back tears were foolish as my chest clenched.

Desperate for any sign of his blessing since I'd begun having feelings for Jake, I'd asked Drew more than once for guidance and received nothing. Until now, that is. I watched the bird flit from one rock to another, singing quietly before it looked at me and flew away, taking my uncertainty with it.

"Thank you, Drew," I whispered as I wiped my tears.

Brushing the dirt from my jeans, I climbed on Dancer. It was time to face the truth I had been running from all along.

"Miss Shelby! We're here!" Campbelle waved furiously as she saw Dancer and I come across the field, her tiny frame bounding from the Jeep as I stopped and jumped down.

I bent to catch her as she ran toward me, returning her hug and grinning wide as she giggled. That drew attention from Max and Dakota, who sprinted in our direction, barking with excitement. When I placed Campbelle on her feet, she was greeted with slobbery kisses, the only thing able to pull my attention from her closing the door to his Jeep.

"Hey." I waved, returning Jake's wide smile as I walked toward him. "How was your flight?"

"Good. Campbelle had a blast. She got a set of wings and told me she's going to be an 'airplane waitress' when she grows up." He chuckled. "Come here."

His large frame engulfed me, and I felt myself melt into his chest as he inhaled me, neither of us willing to release our grip on the other until a light tug on my jeans brought us back to earth.

"Miss Shelby?" Campbelle started, hiding behind me as she gestured toward the porch. "Who are all those people?"

"That's my family, sweetie," I said. "They've been waiting all day to meet you. Would you like to say hello?" I asked, pulling a shy nod from her as I took her hand in mine. "Well, come on. Let's go then."

Campbelle was the perfect little Southern lady, shaking everyone's hands and saying hello. Of course, my sisters decided to grill Jake with questions before he even set foot in the house. Thankfully, my parents stepped in to save us.

"Okay, girls. That's enough," my mom said, waving them off. "Let's get Jake and Campbelle settled into their rooms," my mom said, shooing them away. "Miss Campbelle, would you like to help me bake some cookies?"

"Yes, ma'am." She nodded with a wide grin before glancing up at Jake. "Daddy, can I?"

"Sure, baby girl. Just behave and listen to Mrs. Lansing." He smiled, sticking out his pinky for her to wrap hers around.

"Promise," she said before moving toward my mom.

"Come on, little one." Momma smiled, taking her hand as they disappeared into the kitchen. "We've got a ton of cookies to make. Let's get you all set up."

"Well, I never thought I would be second best to cookies." Jake laughed.

"You haven't tasted my wife's chocolate chip cookies. You will be lower than a snake's belly, son." Daddy chuckled. "If the two of you are interested, we'll be up at the gazebo getting ready for the bonfire and tonight's hayride. We could certainly use a hand."

"Sure." I nodded. "I just want to show Jake around some first, and we'll be up."

"Take your time, honey. I've got the boys and your sisters helping, so we'll be alright." He winked at me before giving Jake a pat on the back. "Welcome to the ranch. Shelby, I'm headed to the barn. I'll take Dancer back with me."

"We look forward to getting to know you better, too, Jake," Sara said.

"Yeah, anyone that can make Shelby smile like that is okay in my book." Jodi nodded, chuckling at my blush.

I gave Jake the official tour, taking extra time in some of the spots on the ranch that meant most to me. Talking to him was easy, like breathing, and by the time we made it up to his room, much of my nervousness had eased.

We took his bags upstairs, and I helped him put a few of Campbelle s things away as he got settled. When he went quiet, I glanced up to find him thinking hard about something, his eyebrows quirking together.

"What is it?"

"Nothing." He shook his head, clearing his throat before giving me a small smile. "It's just been a while since I felt all of this. Being out here, with your family, with you…" he said, meeting my eyes as he reached for my hand, winding his pinky into mine. "Look, I know you're still in college, and our homes are on opposite sides of the coast, but I've gotta be honest with you, Shelby. My heart wants more than your friendship."

His words rendered me speechless for a moment, my nerves coming back full force until I pushed them away.

"What about Campbelle?"

"Campbelle already loves you," he said, his lips quirking up. "She's lost so much in her short life, but I haven't seen her smile at anyone like she smiles at you. Not since Cara was here." He brushed my hair away, searching my eyes before he swallowed hard. "But she's not coming back, Shelby, and neither is Drew. I know how I feel about you, how I think you feel about me."

"I was really scared to get close to you in the beginning," I admitted. "It took me a really long time to open myself to another person, risk getting hurt like that again. I was so convinced I'd never feel for another person what I felt for Drew." I glanced up at him, meeting his eyes. "But then I met you, and you've shown me feelings I've never experienced before with anyone."

Jake leaned in and kissed me, his tongue brushing against mine sending a jolt of electricity through me at the same time I felt my limbs go soft, my heart racing. When he finally pulled away from me, we were both panting as he rested his forehead against mine.

"I'm not sure how much I'm ready for just yet," I confessed, meeting his eyes. "I know I want this, but Drew is the only guy I've ever been with, and he's been gone for a long time."

"We'll take it slow. One day at a time, Shelby. I'm not in any rush," he promised. "Besides, they say your first love is one you never forget, but your last is the one you can't live without."

Gia

Thanksgiving was fun. It was great having everyone around the table, and Nonna kept us all in stitches while she yelled at the TV during the football game. The only thing that sucked was that I wasn't able to be alone with Colin with all this shit going on with Paige and Craig. Don't get me wrong; we had our share of fun, but we had to keep it contained.

The next morning, the guys headed to the office to work on the waterfront property, and Lexi's dad went to see a few of his political friends in Boston. They'd all met for lunch later. As for us girls, we were headed out to shop. It was Black Friday, what I like to call 'chaos and mayhem day,' and I always knew going in that I was guaranteed to see at least one ridiculous fist fight over shit, which was borderline hilarious. Aside from getting breakfast, it was my favorite part of the day.

We'd been at it for a while, the back of the truck quickly filling with our purchases. We'd spread out to cover more ground before lunch, and my shopping list was dwindling fast, giving me a funny sense of accomplishment. It was nearly time to meet the others at Uno's for lunch, and I still hadn't heard from Colin, so while I waited for the girls, I decided to text him.

Hey, sweet cheeks. Just checking in. Miss me?

How'd you guess? My cock and I were just thinking about you.

It hasn't really had me yet lol

Minor technicality.

My ass it is.

I can have your ass? Really?

Not on your life. That's a one-way street, buddy.

Bummer, no pun intended! I have to run, baby. Your brother is being a bossy dick. See you soon. Love you lots.

Love you lots, too.

Chapter Twelve

Theresa

I was right in the middle of picking out some underwear that didn't scream *granny* when Gia texted me, rushing me to meet her for lunch. Hurried was the last thing I needed to feel in that moment. I was overwhelmed as I looked through the lingerie in this place. My drawers had been filled with cotton hi-cuts that I thought were sexy enough until I got there. That place made me feel like a nun.

"This wouldn't cover my eye," I whispered and dropped it back into the bin.

I wasn't sure why I was wasting my time in a place like that. At my age, I had to squeeze my legs together when I sneezed to avoid a catastrophe. My underwear were the least of my worries.

"Theresa, did you find what you wanted?" Lexi asked as she approached me, her arms full of bras and dreaded thongs. "I love this place."

"Their pajamas are very comfortable," I answered, avoiding anything more intimate. No telling what she'd think of me buying more than that in a place like this. "Are you ready to eat lunch? Gia is getting hungry, and God forbid that girl misses a meal."

"Yes," she chuckled. "Cynthia just texted me. She is with Gia now, and they're waiting for us."

"Great, let's get out of here," I said, ushering her toward the exit. "This place is causing me to have a hot flash."

Lexi

After we finished lunch, we were discussing our next plan of attack when my phone pinged with a text from an unknown number. I immediately became anxious until I realized it was Frankie.

Hey babe, it's me. Sorry, I left my phone at the office, so I'm on Julio's phone. Can you come to the waterfront? The crew is here, and they want to start to knock walls down on Monday, but I don't want to screw up the vision you had.

Sure, I am just finishing up lunch. I will be over in a bit. Is that okay?

Of course. We are in the back. Just let yourself in, and I'll see you in a bit.

"Frankie lonely?" Gia laughed.

"No." I smirked. "He needs me to meet them at the waterfront building. The crew is going to start construction on Monday, so he wants to confirm what we are keeping."

"We can drop you off there on our way over to the mall."

"No, it's out of your way." I waved her off. "I will just grab a cab. It's no big deal."

"You sure?"

"Yeah, I got it. I hate to eat and run, but they are waiting for me."

"Okay." Cynthia smiled. "Be careful. We'll see you at the house."

I waved goodbye and headed outside, hailing a cab.

I was grateful for the short ride when we pulled up to the building. I didn't see any of the company trucks but quickly ignored the nerves in my chest, sure they must have parked in the garage. I paid the driver and grabbed my keys, letting myself in. It was dark, the only light coming from the bright red emergency lights that cast a glare over the concrete floors. *That looks like blood*, I thought, ignoring the uneasy feeling that followed as I saw movement coming from the back of the building near the makeshift office.

Eager to get out of the darkness, I dropped my phone and keys into my purse and quickened my steps.

"Frankie?" I called out, the echo of my voice the only response that came.

I released a deep sigh and rounded the corner, jumping when I stepped inside.

Frankie wasn't waiting for me. Instead, I found Craig, tied to a chair, battered and bleeding. His mouth was taped shut, and ropes bound his legs and torso to the chair.

"Oh, my God!" I screamed, dropping my purse as I ran toward him, pushing his slumped shoulders back and checking for a pulse. "Craig? Can you hear me?" I asked frantically as I searched for any signs of life in the dark. "I'm calling an ambulance," I promised, my voice shaking as I reached for my purse, finding nothing but concrete.

"Are you looking for this?" she asked as she slipped from behind a column, my purse in one hand, a gun in the other.

"Paige," I gasped, stumbling back slightly. "What have you done? Where's Frankie?"

"Don't worry. Frankie is just fine," she said, taking a step closer and gesturing toward Craig. "As for him, don't feel too bad. I think we both know he got what he deserved."

"Nobody deserves this, Paige." I shook my head.

"We'll have to agree to disagree." She shrugged. "He used me, then had the balls to say he wanted to teach me a lesson. Little did he know, I would be teaching him one instead."

"Is he dead?" I asked, still slowly backing towards the door.

"I couldn't let you miss all the fun, could I?" she smirked, waving the gun. "No, I thought since you both ruined my life, it would be more fitting that you go together."

"Haven't you heard?" I managed, swallowing hard past the lie I knew was coming, but desperate for anything to get me away from that gun. "Frankie and I are over. He said he wanted you, Pai—"

"Shut your lying whore mouth," she shouted over me, backhanding me into silence. "I've been watching you both, Lexi. Frankie's stuck so far up your ass, it makes me sick," she insisted, pushing me into the chair beside Craig and pointing the gun at my heaving chest. "Now sit down and shut the fuck

194

up. One more word out of you, and I'll shoot you where you stand."

My heart raced. She'd planned it all so perfectly. As she roughly secured me to my seat, my chest began to seize with claustrophobia, making me panic.

"What did I just tell you?" she asked, her eyes staring into mine as the gun pressed back into my chest, the panic coming on full force.

"Paige," I managed, my voice quaking with terror as the tears came. "You don't have to do this. I won't tell—"

"Shut the fuck up!" she shouted, twisting the gun in her hand and hitting me hard against the temple, sending my chair back against the concrete.

She's going to kill me, I thought to myself as I felt my head hit the floor, my vision wavering as she kicked me hard, pulling another sob from my chest. *I'm going to die today.*

I searched for visions of Frankie, the girls, my father, but all that filled my mind was her maniacal laugh before everything finally went black.

Gia

"Hey, can you guys give us a hand, please?" I called out as I stepped inside, juggling my bags.

"Here," Colin said, leaving the guys at the island in the kitchen to rescue me from the sea of bags. "Let me help you, babe."

"Damn," Frankie chuckled as he came down the hallway. "Did Lexi buy out the store?"

"Well, she probably would have if you hadn't cut her day short." I smirked.

"Huh?"

"Well, she was going to go back out with us after lunch, but she had to leave to meet you."

"What are you talking about, Gia? Meet me where?"

"At the friggin' waterfront building, numbnuts."

"We weren't at the waterfront today," he said, his features shifting with his anxiety as he pushed past us. "Lexi?" he called out as he jogged outside before coming back in a moment later, his chest heaving. "Gia, what happened? Where is she?"

"Frankie, she said you texted her to—"

"It wasn't me, Gia. I never texted her to meet me," he admitted as his chest began to heave with fear.

"What's going on?" Jackson asked.

"Where's the PI?" Frankie shouted, spinning to face him.

"I gave him the weekend off. I figured Lexi would be safe with all of us." He shrugged, his eyes shifting once he saw Frankie's face go pale. "What's wrong?"

"We can't find Lexi," I admitted.

"Fuck!" Frankie screamed the anguish in his voice sending a chill through me as my phone chimed with a text.

Your friend is in trouble.
Answer your phone.

Before I could reply, my phone rang, and I knew immediately it was Colleen. I took a step away from the commotion and pulled the phone to my ear.

"Hello?"

"The phone I've been tracking from Frankie's ex is in the same location as Alexis," she said. "They're at an abandoned building by the waterfront."

"Someone call the police," I insisted, looking toward Colin and Angus.

"What's going on?" Jackson demanded. "Where's my daughter?"

"The waterfront," I said, my mind spinning.

"They're already on their way, Moretti, but the signal from her phone hasn't moved," Colleen's voice broke through, making me swallow the sob in my chest. "That only means one of two things."

"Don't," I pleaded in a whisper as my eyes moved to Frankie's, the obvious understanding reaching him as he grabbed his keys, eyes brimming with tears.

"Fuck that," Frankie shook his head. "I'm not waiting for the police."

"I hope she's okay," Colleen offered through the line before the click told me she was gone.

The sound of skidding tires outside told me Frankie was hoping so, too.

Paige

Getting Craig here was the easy part. All I needed was to promise him sex and give him a half-assed apology before his stupid ass showed up. Lexi was a little harder, but when I texted her from my newest burner, pretending to be Frankie, she was just gullible enough to take the bait without question.

Once she was gone and finally out of the picture, Frankie would come crawling back. I just knew it.

A groan from my right pulled me from my thoughts, and I gathered myself, knowing it meant I was one step closer to finishing what I'd started.

"Oh, look who is waking up," I said, kicking Craig's chair.

He winced slightly before widening his eyes and looking around, his words muffled and panicked as his eyes fell on Lexi, who was still out cold.

"Now, now, don't worry," I crooned. "She is not dead. *Yet.*"

She started to stir, so I took a step closer to her and crouched down, gripping her chin.

"How's the head? Does it hurt?" I asked, the sob resting on her lips muffled from the tape as well. "Don't worry. Once I shoot you, you won't feel a thing." As I stood and turned away from them, moving back toward my bag of tricks, their hushed sounds of fear were music to my ears. "Okay you two, it's been real, but I have had enough of the both of you. It's time to say goodbye and good fucking riddance."

Walking over, I decided to pick who died first the fairest way I knew how.

"Eeny, meeny, miny, moe," I sang, waving the gun back and forth between them. "Catch a liar and a hoe."

It was so much fun watching the fear in their eyes as they fought to get free. I internally kicked myself for not having done this sooner. It was arousing.

Stepping forward, I ripped off Craig's tape.

"You fucking bitch," he screamed before gasping for breath. "I will kill you."

"Well, you're tied up and can't do shit, tough guy," I replied. "Before we say goodbye, though, I do have one question, Craig. Does it get you off? Hitting a woman? Making them feel like nothing?" I asked as the memory of his fist crashing against my face all those weeks before flashed in my mind. "Guys like you think their dicks are magic, but let me fill you in on a little something. You are the worst fuck I ever had."

"Stupid fuckin' whore," he ground out, spitting blood at my feet. "You're not going to get away with this."

"But I already have." I smiled, bending closer to him. "You wanted her so badly, you went crazy with jealousy and decided if you couldn't have her, neither would he. You'll stop at nothing until the two of you are together, even if it's in the afterlife." I sighed, lifting the paper. "See? It's all here in your suicide note."

"You're insane," he insisted, pulling a shrug from me.

"Or brilliant," I argued, tracing his bruised jaw with my fingertip. "No one will ever question it was you, Craig."

Craig stared at me for a long moment before finally, he reared back, smashing his head into my nose. Blood exploded everywhere, the blow causing me to fall back and knock the gun from my hand. Trying to get up, I heard a window smash and the room filled with smoke. Choking, my eyes burning, I crawled around, feeling for my gun. Before I could find it, I felt the force of being pushed to the ground followed by yelling, the feel of cold metal wrapping around my wrists making me freeze.

Fuck, I thought as my cheek touched the cold concrete. *I should have killed them sooner.*

Frankie

When I stepped into her room, I found her there sleeping, the familiar sound of the beeping coming from the monitors around her making my throat thick as I moved to the edge of her bed. Her cheek and eye were both bruised, and you could see where the duct tape had left a nasty red mark on her face.

Her eyes flitted open, finding her father and me staring down at her in silence, both of us reaching for her.

"I'm sorry," she managed, her voice strained. "I thought..."

"Shh, honey." Jackson shook his head, squeezing her hand. "Paige is unstable. None of this was your fault."

I ran my eyes over her injuries while they talked, and it wasn't long until the guilt came rushing in, knowing that, once again, she was lying in a hospital bed because of me. The reality of that was enough to have me fighting back emotion.

"Frankie, come here," she said, reaching for me. "I am fine, just a little sore."

"Lexi, I am so sorry, baby," I whispered, wiping the tear slipping down my cheek onto my sleeve as I brushed the hair away from her face. "Please forgive me."

"Forgive you? For what?" she asked, tugging me to sit on the edge of her bed. "You had nothing to do with Paige and her mental instability."

"I tried to get to you," I admitted, resting my head on her neck and holding her close. "I just couldn't get there fast enough."

"You're wrong, Frankie," she whispered as she gazed up at me, searching my features before slowly shaking her head. "You got to me just in time."

Jackson and I sat with Lexi, listening to her version of what happened with Paige, and I had to bite my tongue as she credited Craig with having helped save her life. The thought that an asshole like him could come off as a hero to her in any capacity wasn't something that sat well with me. Not at all.

Before too long, the room began to fill with visitors, and I excused myself to get some air. I'd made it halfway to the elevator when something told me to glance up just in time to find his last name on the door of one of the rooms not far from Lexi's.

My feet slowed, my head telling me to let it go, but my heart won out as pushed the door open and stepped inside.

"What the fuck do you want, Moretti?" he asked when he saw me, his ballsy greeting sounding off as it left him hoarsely.

"Just checking in," I said, glancing around the room before returning my eyes to his. "Lexi told me what you did for her, and it's appreciated, but it also doesn't change anything. Just needed to make sure we were both clear on that."

"You can fucking have her." He waved me off, turning his head to cough before facing me again. "No pussy is worth dying over."

"Maybe." I shrugged. "Might be worth killing over, though. You should probably remember that next time you want to shoot my girlfriend a text."

He stared back at me, the threat hanging thick between us before finally, he nodded his understanding. I turned to leave, nearly to the door before his voice stopped me again.

"One thing I never understood was why she picked you," he admitted, pulling my eyes back to find him sneering at me. "I could have given her exactly the life she was groomed for. Why the hell would she choose average when she could have excellence?"

"Because she's better than the life she was *groomed for*, asshole." I shook my head. "And she needed a real man to help her see that, not an entitled little bitch like you."

Gia

Two months later

I'd been sitting beside the window in my bedroom, wrapped in a blanket as I took in the snow falling outside. It was pretty, and I'd always loved it as a kid, but as an adult, it was a real pain in the ass. One saving grace was having classes canceled, giving me the chance to lounge in my pajamas all day and binge on Netflix.

I got lost in my thoughts and, like usual, they eventually drifted back to everything that had happened with Paige. I was so grateful that Lexi was okay, that my best friend had come through on the other side safe. My only regret was that I never had a chance to really thank Colleen for saving her.

"We need a fucking vacation." I sighed, resting my head against the cold window. My thoughts trailed off in a different direction then, and it wasn't long until I was lifting my phone to call Frankie.

"Gia, this better be fucking important. I am up to my ass in snow trying to plow out my sites. I don't have time to chit-chat," he yelled over the sound of the plow scraping against the pavement.

"Oh, shut up, dick face. I am your only sister, and when I call, you pick up for me just like you do for Lexi. Besides, I will make it fast. I was thinking about going to Aruba for Spring Break. Sun, drinks, sand in your ass crack, the whole nine yards. Thoughts?"

"Not alone, you're not. That Natalie girl that disappeared out there was your age. There's no fucking way I'm letting you go by yourself," he insisted, yelling something at Mikey and Joey before returning his attention to me. "Besides, I thought you had a boyfriend. Why the hell are you planning a trip to Aruba by yourself?"

"I'm not. I meant all of us, and I'm calling him next." I rolled my eyes, laughing as I glanced out the window and watched Samantha, Stacy, and Beth trying to maneuver the ice-covered steps. *Rookies.* "Anyway, what are you freaking out over? I'm talking about Aruba, where all the old people go to get more wrinkles, not Daytona Beach, for Christ's sake."

"Hey! We want to go to Aruba!" Mikey yelled from the truck in the background. "My balls are frozen and need to be defrosted, for fuck sake, this shit is getting old fast."

"Mikey, the last thing I need is a vision of your balls stuck to your legs." I rolled my eyes. "But yes, you can come, too, if your boss allows it."

Outside, Samantha fell on her perfect little ass, her minions struggling to help get her back up as I began cackling with laughter.

"What's so funny, Gia? You want to see my nutcicle?" Mikey laughed. "That boyfriend of yours not cutting it anymore, baby?"

"No, the girl you've been secretly banging across the street just took a digger and is covered in snow and shit." I chuckled. "It looks like her ass might be out of commission for a while."

"Shut up, Gia," he said defensively. "She isn't that bad, she's just misunderstood."

"Turn them upside down, and they all look the same, right Mikey?" I teased. "Anyway, enough about that. While you boys are busy plowing something," —I snorted suggestively— "I'll call Colin to see if he's up for it. I'll let you know what he says."

We hung up, and I sent Colin a text asking him to call me when he could. I hoped he said yes; this long-distance shit was getting really hard, and our constant failed attempts at sex hadn't helped anything. It seemed like no matter how hard we tried, something ridiculous happened, and I was seriously on the verge of losing my shit.

I heard movement in the kitchen telling me that the girls were finally awake, and I made my way downstairs, smiling when I saw them.

"Thank God we don't have class today," Lexi said, clinking her spoon next to the side of her cup. "I had a test in business, and I needed a few more days to study."

"Me, too," Shelby agreed as she shuffled across the hardwood floors. "I could use a break. Between school and the stable, I am exhausted."

"There you are," Lexi said as she approached the window I was standing beside in the living room. "What are you doing?"

"Watching these three assholes trying to shovel their way out of the snow," I said, pointing to the idiots outside before turning to them. "Hey, I'm waiting for Colin to call me back, but I want to run something by you two."

"What's up?" Shelby asked.

"Well, last year, we spent Spring Break here in Boston, but I thought it'd be fun to go to Aruba this year," I said, hoisting myself onto the arm of the couch. "What do you think? Sun and fun?"

"I'd love to, but I'm going to Montana. Mike's proposing to Jodi, and Christian's going to see Sara so that we can all be there when it happens," Shelby said, shaking her head at the stooges outside. "Besides, Jake wouldn't be able to come. He's got Campbelle."

"Shit, that's right. I forgot you mentioned going home," I said, making a sad face. "Well, that blows. It won't be as much fun without you."

"Y'all should still go." She waved me off, sipping her coffee. "Just promise to take lots of pics."

"We will," Lexi promised, pulling her in for a side hug, all of us simultaneously roaring with laughter as the plow drove by and threw muddy snow all over the girls outside.

While I waited to hear from Colin, Lexi and I researched everything online for the bulk of the morning. By lunchtime, everything was planned down to the penny. and I decided I'd been a patient girlfriend long enough. While Lexi called Frankie and filled him in, I dialed Colin, loving the butterflies that still filled my chest when I heard his voice.

"Hey gorgeous," he said, the noise from heavy equipment from the lumber yard in the background.

"Hey yourself, handsome."

"What trouble are you up to today, baby?"

"I want to go to Aruba for Spring Break," I said, looking down at my nails like I didn't care although I was silently chomping at the bit. "If you're interested, I guess you can come with me."

"Aruba, huh?" he said, his voice amused. "Well, I might be. You'll have to tell me what's in it for me. Is everyone coming?"

"No. Shelby's going home to Montana for her sister's engagement, so she and Jake won't be joining us."

"Well, that sucks. It's too bad she won't make it," he said, chuckling after a second. "You know, it's funny. Jake came by the office this morning, talking up a storm about her and asking if I'd be going to Boston anytime soon. I guess he's looking to take a trip up that way."

"Really?" I asked. "That's sweet. Shelby will be excited."

"Yeah, I think those two are perfect together," he confessed. "They found their soulmates, just like we did."

Chapter Thirteen

Gia

Spring Break Aruba had finally arrived, and I was bouncing for joy knowing I would be with Colin in just a few short hours.

Getting on our flight, I once again drew the short straw and had Mikey and Joey on each side. Miami would be different, though, because I knew Colin would be sitting with me in first class. He'd upgraded our tickets for some privacy. When Frankie heard, he did the same—no way was Lexi going to ride coach.

The flight was uneventful. We watched a few movies, and I read a great book, *Sprung* by Kate Benson, that had me laughing the entire trip. I had also loaded up two more authors to read on the trip, Sapphire Knight and Nina Levine. These ladies wrote hot, horny, Alpha-men who rocked your world. What a combo—hot men, hot sun while lying next to my man. Orgasm city.

Landing in Miami, I was chomping at the bit to see Colin. When we stepped off the ramp into the waiting area, he was already waiting for me, the goofiest smile on his lips before he stalked toward me as if I were his prey. He scooped me into his arms and kissed me until Frankie ruined the moment.

"Okay, partner." He laughed. "Let her go before you get her pregnant."

I'd never flown in first class before, but now that I had, I believed it was a must for everyone at least once. We spent our time wrapped in warm blankets, eating warm nuts, and sipping champagne. It was pure heaven.

After we took off and were settled, Colin decided to play peek-a-boo with his pecker. Pretending we were asleep, I carefully placed my hand under the blanket and stroked him while he closed his eyes and enjoyed the ride. When he was finished, he decided to reciprocate and slipped his hand down my yoga pants, moving my underwear to the side while he made my flight one I would never forget.

When the pilot announced to the flight crew it was time to prepare the cabin for landing, I looked out the window to find aqua blue water all around us. It was beautiful, and I couldn't wait to float my ass in it.

Downtown was busy with people shopping and enjoying the casinos. I was like a little kid in a candy store watching Louis Vuitton, Ralph Lauren, and Coach signs as we headed toward the resort we'd be staying at. One look over at Lexi, and I knew she felt the same way, her eyes taking stock of all the stores she couldn't wait to hit as well. We gave each other a discreet high-five, the boys completely oblivious to our plan. This would be the best vacation ever.

After checking in, Frankie and Lexi headed to their suite with plans to meet us back at the bar at happy hour, claiming they were *tired* and *wanted to lay down*. Meanwhile, Mikey and Joey were already off scoping out the chicks.

Colin and I were finally alone.

We made our way toward our room, the heavy silence between us unusual, and it was obvious that we were both nervous. My thoughts began to drift to our disastrous track record, me getting stuck sleeping with my mom over New Year's, the *just the tip cockblock*, and the now-infamous *gum incident*. By the time we made it to our door, and Colin had pushed it open, I was on the verge of a panic attack.

He stepped inside, setting our bags down while I waited at the door for instructions like an idiot until he finally turned and faced me.

"Colin, I'm nervous," I confessed, biting my lip as the butterflies swirled in my stomach.

"Come here, Gia" he ordered quietly, his voice low and rugged. I moved toward him, his palm brushing my waist making my mouth go dry as he bent to trace my jaw with his lips. "Short of an earthquake or a tsunami, I think this might actually happen for us," he husked as he dipped his head lower, sinking his lips into my neck. "Don't be nervous, baby."

My nerves faded with every touch, the butterflies still there but quickly turning to something different altogether.

His hands moved lower, finding the hem of my shirt and pulling it over my head. His eyes locked on the red lace underneath before he buried his face in my chest, lapping and sucking as he pushed my yoga pants down.

"Mother of God, I've hit the lottery," he whispered as he saw the matching thong that barely covered me. He lifted me into his arms before tossing me onto the bed.

With a breathy laugh, I scooted back until I touched the headboard and watched him pull his shirt off, revealing his six pack and the dark trail of hair that led to the motherload. Once he was naked, he climbed slowly up the mattress, grabbing my ankles and pulling me down beneath him, making me gasp.

"You smell delicious," he groaned as he began sucking on my earlobe, his tongue trailing down my neck.

I could feel his dick throbbing against my stomach, and I reached between us, stroking him until he gently pushed me away.

"I'm a man with very little restraint right now," he admitted. "You're gonna have to give me a little more time to explore before you start trying to set me off, baby."

I giggled quietly to myself, my laughter fading as he pushed my bra away, making a feast of me until I was lifting my hips in desperation, seeking relief for the friction building between my thighs.

"Not yet, my impatient little kitty," he teased as he began dragging his tongue down my belly, kissing the inside of my thighs until it was unbearable.

"Colin, please," I whimpered, my breath leaving me in a pant. "Baby, you gotta give me something before I explode."

He released a low hum of satisfaction, knowing he was turning me inside out before finally kissing his way down the middle of my thong, teasing the lace with his teeth before pushing it to the side and covering me with his mouth. He licked and sucked until I couldn't breathe, his no touching rule flying quickly out the window as I grabbed his head, desperate for more. When he finally came up for air and looked at me, my limbs were jelly, and his lips were holding the widest, wettest grin I'd ever seen in my life.

"Holy fuck!" I blurted, my chest still heaving as he rose over me, his lips trailing over my breasts along the way.

"Just the beginning," he promised, lingering on my breasts before his lips were hovering over mine. "I'm about to give you the fucking of your life," he teased, his cock pressing against my opening, the tip thick and swollen as it grazed against me. "When I'm through with you, you'll be so marked up, you'll think my dick was still buried inside you, Gia."

Like radar, Maggie knew her day had finally come as she wiggled against him. Colin pushed in an inch and pulled back out, leaving me empty. He was teasing me relentlessly, the dance going on long enough that eventually, I couldn't take it anymore. I gripped the globes of his ass and raised my hips, pulling him inside me all at once. His dick hit that spot that stole my breath, his chest releasing a low growl as I clenched around him while he drove into me, riding me in slow, methodical moves.

Our lustful dance began slowly, but it wasn't long until he flipped me onto my stomach and pressed his body against mine, placing his dick between my legs. I started to panic. I was a one-hole kind of girl, and that was sacred ground.

"Relax, Gia," he whispered as he moved down my back, stopping at the top of my ass. "I won't touch that. Not *yet*."

Reaching for my hips, he lifted me in the air, my fingers clenching the pillow as he pushed back inside me, taking me to an entirely new level of ecstasy.

"Baby, fuck," he hissed. The low moan leaving his chest was all it took to send me over the edge and let go completely.

I pushed back, slamming my ass into him, taking him as deep as I could. He pushed me to the edge again and again until finally, his hand gripped my shoulder, both of us falling apart as little white stars began shooting in front of my eyes.

My legs were shaking, his breathing ragged as we collapsed onto the bed. Colin wrapped his arm around my waist, securing the connection we'd finally formed.

"Holy fucking shit," I panted. "That was totally worth the wait."

His lips pressed into my hair, and he stroked my stomach with his fingers, finally whispering the only words he had the energy left to say.

"I love you, Gia."

Lexi

Frankie and I decided to put the Jacuzzi in our room to good use after the long flight. Looking out over the balcony, I watched the Jet Ski's shoot across the blue waters as the parasailers danced in the sky, lost in the beauty of Aruba. My thoughts began to run away with me as I felt two muscular arms wind around my stomach, pulling me into his chest.

It was the first time since my attack that I'd ever felt completely relaxed.

"What are you thinking about?"

"Us," I admitted, glancing out over the beach and watching the waves quietly crash against the shore. "We've been through so much as a couple, and nothing has come between us."

"You and I have grown together through circumstances most would have walked away from, making what we have unbreakable," he said kissing my temple. "Love will always prevail."

"I love you, Frankie."

"I love you more," he said, bending down taking my lips.

Grabbing me by my ass, he lifted me up as if I weighed less than a feather, and I wrapped my legs around him, holding on tight until he gently sat me on the bed. I leaned back against the mattress while he stood over me, pulling his shirt off before he pushed my legs apart, rubbing his dick against me.

"Do you want to play? Or do you want to hit the Jacuzzi?" he asked, continuing to tease me.

"What do you think?" I smirked, pulling him on top of me. "I want to play."

"Good," he said, lifting my shirt and leaning down to suck on my nipple. "I hate to let a good hard-on go to waste."

"God, you make me crazy," I said, grabbing him and stroking him while he pumped in my hand, still sucking on my breasts like a starving man.

Sitting back on his heels, his hands roamed up and down my body, zeroing in on my jeans. He slowly unbuttoned my pants while kissing me, only stopping to pull them off and toss them onto the floor.

Returning to me, he smashed his lips on mine, sweeping his tongue across my lips before he slipped his tongue into my mouth, our tongues dancing together. Frankie lifted his body over mine once again allowing me to stroke him while he pumped my hand. Unable to hold on any longer I guided his cock into me and with one swift push, he was inside me deep. Frankie took control, setting the rhythm and pace, taking me along for the ride before finally, we were both crashing, falling over the edge.

We laid there, catching our breath for a long while before his lips brushed my ear and he pulled me closer.

"I finally found my happy," he whispered.

"Hmm," I hummed. "So did I, baby."

Gia

After another round with Colin, he slept peacefully beside me. My self-doubt started to kick in lying next to this gorgeous man. Why would he want a girl like me?

"Gia," he muttered his voice heavy with sleep. "Stop."

"Stop what?"

"Letting your head run away with you."

"I'm not!" I lied.

"Baby, I know you better than you think, and I can tell you're getting all caught up in some bullshit right now," he called me out as he rolled onto his back, pulling me against his chest. "Aside from you today, and my mother on her deathbed, I've never told a woman I loved them. I meant it, or I wouldn't have said it."

"God," I groaned dramatically, kissing his jaw. "I really hate when you get all sweet and shit. Come on." I sat up, tugging at his arm until he squinted, one eye open. "Let's get dressed and go to the bar."

"Let's stay here," he disagreed, his hands moving lower down my back.

"I'm not going to be able to sit right for the rest of the week as it is," I argued, making him chuckle. "And I'm starving. Feed me."

"Fine," he surrendered, giving me a kiss on the forehead before he released me. "I guess I'll be a good boyfriend and let you rest your vagina while you eat."

"Gee, thanks." I rolled my eyes.

"Don't get used to it," he teased, smacking my ass. "I've got plans for you in that water," he said, slipping out of bed and walking toward the bathroom, my eyes glued to his ass. *Oh yeah. I'm tappin' that.* "Get dressed. There's a rack of Balashi and Dushi Aruba's with our names on it."

Colin and I were the first two at the bar, which also meant we were two drinks ahead of everyone. With all the sex and lack of food in my system, I was already starting to feel it. The first to join us were Mikey and Joey. As they came around the corner, I nearly choked on my drink when I saw who was with them.

"What the hell is this shit, Mikey?" I demanded, giving him the stink eye.

"Samantha and Beth are here on Spring Break, Gia. Get over it."

"I know you and I haven't seen eye to eye," Samantha said, showing her balls as she came to a stop in front of me. "I apologize for that. I would like to start over again."

Looking down at her extended paw, I laughed.

"You want to start over, do you? Well, how about this. You apologize to Shelby for treating her like shit, and then come talk to me."

"Shelby and I are just fine. I've already apologized to her, and she's been giving me riding lessons for the past two months. We've moved on, so now it's your turn."

It seemed our little cowgirl had become quite the secret keeper. I'd be sure to ask her about it when I talked to her later. She had some explaining to do.

"Fine." I shrugged. "I'll call a truce, but you step out of line one time and fuck with my friends again, and I'll knock you on your skinny little ass. Am I clear?"

"Crystal."

Lexi and Frankie showed up a while later, looking confused as to why I was standing next to Samantha taking a shot instead of punching her. Samantha did the right thing and apologized for her behavior to Lexi, and we began to all relax.

The bartender, Ruben, told us to take our drinks down to the water and watch the sunset so we could see it sizzle on the water. We saw beautiful colors of red, orange, pink, and dark purple as the sun disappeared for another day, taking a little of the stress from the past year with it.

It was a perfect ending to a perfect day.

Colin and I walked the beach hand in hand in the moonlight, stopping to kiss while taking in the beauty of the island. Tomorrow we were taking a cruise on the Mi Dushi pirate boat which had a rope swing off the mast, snorkeling, and their famous rum punch. This island would always have a special place in my heart. It's where I gave myself to a man who truly loved me.

As promised, every single part of me was sore in the best way the next morning as I woke up and stretched out next to Colin. Being the perfect girlfriend, I quietly snuck out of the room to get us coffee and fruit before we met everyone for breakfast. On the way back, I passed Samantha who was wearing the infamous *walk of shame* ensemble. I could only hope for her sake that she wasn't foolish enough to think Mikey would fall in love with her. He was more of a hit it and quit it kind of guy.

"Hi, Gia."

"Hey, Sam. I am still a little hung over and haven't had my coffee yet," I said, trying to get to the coffee urn and not be rude. Just because we'd taken a few shots together, I didn't need her thinking I was going to be her new BFF.

"It's okay. I am just heading back to my room. Mikey invited me to go with you guys on the boat, so I need my clothes and have to check on Beth. Joey brought her back to our room last night while I stayed with Mikey."

"Well, if it makes you feel any better, I'm sure Joey is probably sleeping on the floor, and Beth is tucked safely in bed. He isn't like that at all. He's a really decent guy. She will be fine." My words seemed to make her feel better about having ditched her friend for sex, giving me an out I jumped at. "Well, I have to get this coffee and fruit back to my room. See you in a little while."

When I made it back to our room, I looked inside and was surprised to find the bed empty. I finally found Colin in a lounge chair outside, sitting silently.

"Hey, sleepyhead." I smiled, sitting beside him. "I brought you coffee."

"Thanks," he said, giving me a small smile before taking a sip.

His tone was clipped, something I wasn't used to. For some reason, ever since we'd slept together, Colin had acted like he wasn't sure what to do with me, and a part of me wondered if he regretted everything that had happened between us.

As afraid as I was to find out I was right, the nagging feeling was one I knew I wouldn't shake until we talked about it.

"Are you okay?" I asked as I looked over at him. "You seem upset about something."

"You weren't here when I woke up," he said. "I thought you'd left me."

"I went to get coffee, Colin." I smirked nervously. "I didn't leave the country."

"As long as you're in my bed, you don't ever just get up and leave," he insisted.

"Are you shitting me?"

"No, I'm not shitting you, Gia. How would you feel if I let you wake up like that? No note, just gone?" he asked. "Like it or not, I love you. If I have to say it to you a million times a day for the rest of my life, I'll do it if that's what it takes to get it through your head, babe, but when we're in bed, you don't leave. Not like that. Am I clear?"

The emotion in his words not only helped me understand, it kind of blew me away. I'd never mattered that much to anyone, and the more I thought about it, I felt exactly the same way about him.

"Yeah, okay." I nodded, reaching for his hand. "I'm sorry."

"Come here," he said, pulling me into his lap with a smirk. "Give me a kiss, you little shit."

"You're bossy," I said, doing as I was told. "You're also pretty cute."

Our day was spent jumping off the rope swing, laying on the deck and of course, drinking. We visited Baby Beach, a lagoon where you could float, snorkel, or just bask in the sun. What I didn't realize was that in Aruba, bathing suit tops were optional, so when we stepped onto the beach, there were tits as far as the eye could see. While the boys started off like giggling little idiots, enjoying the scenery, all it took was the threat of us pulling our tops off to cut that shit quick.

Over the course of the next week, we toured the island. On our last day, we bar hopped on an open-air bus, ending the day toasting our final sunset with champagne and our closest friends.

"A toast to love," Colin said, wrapping his arm around me as he held his glass out in a toast. "May each kiss be sweet and cause your heart to skip a beat."

"Cheers!"

I'd always heard Aruba was called *one happy island.*

Now, I knew why.

Epilogue

Two years later

Gia

The girls and I stepped out of the car in our caps and gowns, paying our respects to the one person who couldn't be here with us today.

Nonna.

It had been a year since she'd passed away in her sleep, leaving a hole in all our hearts that we knew immediately would never heal. She lived her life loving her family and her beloved New England Patriots, always saying what was on her mind and never regretting a word of it.

Her surgery didn't give her the longevity we had hoped, but it gave us a little more time. The morning we lost her, I walked into her room where she laid in her bed, her rosary beads in her hand. I knew right away she was gone. She died the way she wanted, saying her prayers and with dignity. I gently sat beside her and held her hand as I told her how much I loved her. I cried knowing she would never see us walk down the aisle or hold our children, instead remembered through photographs and all the stories we would someday tell them.

Her funeral was a testament to how many lives she'd touched. People came from all over wearing their favorite Patriots jerseys, paying respects to New England's biggest fan. Her casket was adorned with Superbowl banners and her number twelve jersey with *Nonna* embroidered on the back.

I instantly knew life would never be the same once we said goodbye to her, but I felt comfort in knowing she was smiling down on us now. We had a kickass guardian angel protecting us.

Lexi and Shelby stood behind me as I knelt and placed a rose at the base of the stone.

"Nonna, there isn't a day I don't miss you," I whispered. "Some days, I feel like I can't even breathe, but I know you are with us today and will help guide us through our next journey. We love you, and we miss you."

I sat there with her for a moment, thinking about her legacy and the time I was lucky to share with her. I stood and watched Shelby and Lexi bend down and place their roses next to mine.

Holding hands, we walked back to the car, ready to close this chapter in our lives and turn the page to the next one.

After the graduation ceremony, we all gathered at Ma's to celebrate. Over the past four years, our families had become close, and it was amazing to have everyone here to share this moment. As the party was kicking off, Frankie called us all over to Nonna's bench, waiting for us to settle before he raised his glass.

"I would like to propose a toast to Lexi, Gia, and Shelby. You three have accomplished something that some could only dream. Be proud of your accomplishments, mentor others, and always pay it forward."

"Salute."

"Now that I have everyone's attention, I have one more thing to add," he continued, his voice quieting the chit chat around us. "Lexi, can you come here, please?"

She took a step forward, and he led her to the bench, setting her glass to the side as he gestured for her to sit. She looked up at him, her confusion pulling a laugh from Frankie before he took a deep breath and finally, bent on one knee in front of her.

"Lexi, you are my best friend," he said as he took her hand, ignoring the gasps of surprise around us as he stared up at her in adoration. "I never knew I could love anyone as much as I love you. We have been through hell and back, but our love has only grown stronger. Now, I only want to give you a lifetime of happiness," he said, reaching into his pocket and pulling out a black box. "Will you marry me?"

It was only a moment before she covered her mouth in shock, crying tears of joy like I'd never seen, not just in her, but in anyone.

"Yes," she nodded, resting her hands on his jaw and pressing her lips to his. "Oh, my God, Frankie! Yes!"

When she pulled away, he took her hand and slipped the two-carat, princess cut diamond onto her finger before pulling her close and kissing her once more while we all cheered.

It was perfect.

Ma wiped her tears of joy, and Jackson smiled widely while the rest of us continued to cheer loudly. I was so grateful to share this moment with all the people who mattered most.

"Don't worry, baby," Colin whispered as I brushed my own tears.

"About what?" I asked, staring into his emerald eyes, butterflies still taking over after all this time.

"When it's our turn, it'll be something you'll never forget," he promised, kissing my hair. "You'll see."

His words made my heart skip a beat, and as I stared up at the clear, blue sky, I smiled.

"Thank you, Nonna," I whispered. "Thank you."

Acknowldgments

There are so many people to thank for supporting me with this series.

First and foremost, my readers. Thank you from the bottom of my heart for taking the time to leave a review or send me a message. It means the world to an author to see how their words have left a mark.

Mary Jo G, thank you so much for being my second set of eyes. I love you to the moon and back.

To my PA, Crystal Matz, thank you for pimping and promoting each week in the blogs. Your hard work and dedication mean the world to me.

Charlie, I can't even put into words how grateful I am to you for helping pimp and promote the story.

To my Beta girls, Crystal, Lynn, Phyl, Kate, Shanna and Charlie. Thanks for your honesty and feedback, it made a world of difference.

Sapphire Knight, I am so blessed having such a great friend like you to talk to and lean on for support. Thank you for always being there.

Check out Sapphire on Facebook https://www.facebook.com/AuthorSapphireKnight/

Last, but never least is my editor, friend, and mentor, Kate Benson. I couldn't have done this without you. I am not going to get all mushy, but just know you have a special place in my heart. Thank you for helping me get the words right and making my story special.

Check Kate out on Facebook https://www.facebook.com/katebensonauthor/

A special shout out to:

Nativesons Designs. Sean, I love you. Thank you so much for my beautiful cover. You did a great job, and I love it.

PK Designs Editing and Graphics. I may have written the words, but you made them beautiful. Thank you.

Give Me Books for promoting my story. Your support means the world to me.

Chasing Sophie Publications. Kate, you already know how I feel about you. I love you and thank you.

All the blogs who shared and helped promote this book. Thank you!

About the Author

P. Marie lives in a small town outside of Boston, where she was born and raised. While she is a corporate girl during the day, she has become both a writer and blogger by night. She owes her success to her mother, who taught her that if you believe in yourself, you can achieve anything. If you want more of the crew check out:

Welcome to Beantown
Books2Read:
https://www.books2read.com/welcometobeantown
Amazon: http://amzn.to/2j2rTtv
Nook: http://bit.ly/2kfCTke
Kobo: http://bit.ly/2kqpNjC
iBooks: http://apple.co/2kpxEly

Back in Beantown
Back in Beantown (#2)
Books2Read: https://books2read.com/BackInBeantown
Amazon: http://amzn.to/2vp8V28
Nook: http://bit.ly/2t26phr
Kobo: http://bit.ly/2voxHiL
iBooks: http://apple.co/2voMg62

A Boston Belles Novel
Goodreads: http://bit.ly/2dse6L9

Stalking her at:

Facebook: https://www.facebook.com/pmarieauthor/
Goodreads: http://bit.ly/2iPD6xy
Twitter: https://twitter.com/nennbb
P. Marie Boston Belles: http://bit.ly/2Dtaa4Y

Made in the USA
Lexington, KY
15 September 2018